"Rarely does a book come around that rips you from head to toe, exposing your deepest woundedness and forcing you to confront the inner demons you've skirted for years. But that's what happens when you read *To Own a Dragon*. This penetrating book addresses a crisis affecting millions of men—namely, the plight of guys who grow up without a dad in the home. Whether you grew up without a dad or you just want to be a better father, you'll want to own this Dragon. It's a powerful reminder about the critical role dads play and our need for the Father above."

—*New Man* magazine

"Don Miller is a gifted writer. In the span of two paragraphs, he can have you doubled over in laughter and then on the brink of tears. While he aims his words directly at those who have felt the pain of not having a father to guide them, he's also talking to me as a dad, giving me a not-so-subtle reminder of the awesome responsibility I have for my kids. If you couldn't get enough of Don's style in *Blue Like Jazz* or *Searching for God Knows What*, wait until you see what he's done with John MacMurray in *To Own a Dragon*. They shoot from the hip and from the heart—and don't miss."

—ERNIE JOHNSON JR., studio host, NBA on TNT

"This book is vintage Miller. He once again opens up his heart and lets it bleed with honesty."

—TIM CASH, former pro baseball player; national director of Unlimited Potential, Inc.

To Own a Dragon
REFLECTIONS ON GROWING UP **WITHOUT A FATHER**

DONALD MILLER
& JOHN MACMURRAY

NAVPRESS®

BRINGING TRUTH TO LIFE

The Navigators is an international Christian organization. Our mission is to reach, disciple, and equip people to know Christ and to make Him known through successive generations. We envision multitudes of diverse people in the United States and every other nation who have a passionate love for Christ, live a lifestyle of sharing Christ's love, and multiply spiritual laborers among those without Christ.

NavPress is the publishing ministry of The Navigators. NavPress publications help believers learn biblical truth and apply what they learn to their lives and ministries. Our mission is to stimulate spiritual formation among our readers.

ISBN 1-57683-731-9

Cover Design: The DesignWorks Group, Tim Green, thedesignworksgroup.com
Cover Photo: Getty Images, Jason Hetherington
Illustrations by Adam Haynes.
Creative Team: Nicci Hubert, Don Simpson, Darla Hightower, Arvid Wallen,
    Pat Reinheimer

Some of the anecdotal illustrations in this book are true to life and are included with the permission of the persons involved. All other illustrations are composites of real situations, and any resemblance to people living or dead is coincidental.

Library of Congress Cataloging-in-Publication Data

Miller, Donald, 1971-
  To own a dragon : reflections on growing up without a father / Donald
Miller and John MacMurray.
     p. cm.
  ISBN 1-57683-731-9
  1. Fatherhood--Religious aspects--Christianity. 2. Miller, Donald,
1971- I. MacMurray, John. II. Title.
  BV4529.17.M55 2006
  248.8'421--dc22
                                         2006000866

Printed in the United States of America

1 2 3 4 5 6 / 10 09 08 07 06

DEDICATED TO MEN WHO ARE
MENTORING YOUNGER MEN

CONTENTS

PROLOGUE

I've never written a prologue before, but near as I can tell this is where an author explains a book's shortcomings and asks the reader's kindness. This book has many deficiencies, and I am sorry for them. If it helps you to know I wrote the book in one sitting, on a plane leaving Pittsburgh for Los Angeles, I would ask you to keep this in mind. It's not true, but the thought may help.

I also want to say something to the women who will attempt this book. I am delighted you have chosen to join us, and you are more than welcome, though you must kindly accept my apology for aiming the text at less agreeable creatures. It is not that I think women are less affected by the absence of a father, only that I have relied on personal experience. I think we would all agree inking a stroke toward the feminine would have been a financial move rather than a personal exploration of the issue. I might have sold more books but it would have exposed the fact I know nothing about women, save their lovely smell. So, the decision to target a male audience will explain the simple vocabulary, short chapters, and bathroom humor. I only hope when you come across the latter, you will be honored to remember I would never have been so offensive if I'd known you were in the room.

A note should be made about the voice of the book and the way John and I went about it. I lived with John and his family for four years, and learned a great deal while I was there. In thinking about what to say to young men who grew up without fathers, I relied on many of the principles I learned from John. In putting the book together, then, John and I would talk through issues and I would write each chapter with these conversations in mind. The voice is mine, but the wisdom is his.

That said, this book has been healing for me to get on paper. A writer learns more from what he writes than the reader, and often applies the perspectives after the book is written. We're a depraved group in that way. As for the healing, I hope something like my experience in writing this book happens to you in the reading. It means a great deal to John and me that you would want to spend time with us, and we are grateful.

Donald Miller

Chapter One

THE REPLACEMENTS:
WE'VE GOT MEN ON THE GROUND

I n the absence of a real father, I had a cast of characters
that were at times hilarious, pitiful, perfect, kind, and
wise.

Here they are:

My first father was a black man on television who wore
bright argyle sweaters. He lived in New York or Chicago, I
can't remember which. He was incredibly intelligent, and
had a knockout wife. I'm talking about Bill Cosby. When
I was a kid, I wanted to be Theo Huxtable. I liked the way
Theo dressed. I liked that he was confident with women
and even though he didn't make good grades still felt good
about himself, and he had good-looking sisters who were

both older and younger and who always gave him encouragement and advice about life, along with safe male-female tension. I liked that Bill Cosby had money, too, tons of cash and certain philosophies about saving and spending that gave the family a sense of security, which turned his knockout wife on and had her singing slow, sultry blues melodies to him from the bed while he brushed his teeth in the master bathroom. Bill Cosby never panicked about small things, he never got worked up about broken windows or cereal on the floor, and if he did get worked up, it was more like a comedy routine than a drunken rampage. He also laughed at himself, which was endearing, and I would sit in front of the little black-and-white television in my room and live vicariously through the made-up life of the Huxtables, who had celebrity guests coming through the house every few episodes to play the trombone or tap-dance.

My mom was great, don't get me wrong, but the only guests we ever had at our house were from the singles group at church, and none of them ever whipped out a trombone to play "When the Saints Go Marching In" or tap-danced in the living room or recited a piece of epic prose about the underground railroad on which "our people" had traversed from oppression and slavery to freedom. Our guests, rather, ate meatballs on paper plates and talked bitterly about their ex-husbands.

I also liked the fact that, on *The Cosby Show*, there was never any serious conflict. When Theo graduated from college, for example, the conflict simply involved the family only having ten tickets to the graduation ceremony. Bill wanted to invite the whole neighborhood. All the ladies kept looking at him and shaking their heads, because Bill Cosby's love for his family was always causing him to make a mess of things. They would shake their heads and laugh, and he would make a funny face, and Theo would throw his hands up, look at the ceiling, and roll his eyes while exclaiming *Gosh, Dad!* . . . and I would roll over backward on the floor and look up at the ceiling, sigh, and say under my breath, *Black people have it perfect.*

White people had interesting fathers, too, but nothing to make a sitcom about. When I was growing up my friend Tom had a father, and I learned from this that a real father doesn't have jazz singers over to perform in the living room before dinner, and that real families with fathers don't lip-sync Motown tunes or give speeches at college graduations. Rather, real fathers, at least at Tom's house, clean guns while watching television, weed-eat the lawn with one hand while holding a beer in the other, and squeeze their wife's butt in the kitchen while she is cooking dinner. And because of Tom's father, and because I watched *The Cosby Show* with the devotion of a Muslim, I came to believe a man was supposed to be around the house to arm and disarm weapons, make sexual advances on the matriarch, perform long and colorful ad-libs with children about why they should clean their room and, above all, always face the camera, even if the entire family has to sit on one side of the table during dinner.

MY MOTHER WAS the only female father in my Boy Scout troop, and God knows she tried. But the truth is she had no idea what she was doing. We had a pinewood derby car race where you had to carve a car out of a block of wood, then set it on a ramp and race some other guy with a pinewood car. I came in dead last. The night we made the cars my mom dropped me off at the den mother's house and trusted the fathers who were in the garage making their sons' cars to also help make mine. They didn't. I didn't care. I just wanted to drill holes in the cement driveway with a cordless drill. I don't even think my car had wheels when it came time to race, just a lot of WD-40 on the bottom of a block of wood and a stripe down the side like that car in *The Dukes of Hazzard*.

On race night, with a hundred Boy Scouts standing around and two hundred moms and dads standing around with them, my block of wood slid down the ramp at quarter-speed and came to a sudden stop right about the time the ramp gave way to flatness. Everybody got quiet. I just stood there with my hands on my hips, shaking my head saying, *That General Lee, always breaking down.* My mom was terribly upset about the incident, but I didn't realize it at the time. We picked up the General Lee and left early, right after my mother had sharp words for the men in our den group, who spoke sharply back to her about a driveway full of drill holes.

Mom kept trying. She asked our landlord's son, who was a pothead, if he would take me to the Boy Scout father-and-son campout. His name was Matt, and he drove a red Volkswagen bug and listened to Lynyrd Skynyrd tapes and ended every sentence with the phrase, "Do you know what I mean, dude?" He was pretty cool, but I think he felt out of place around the other fathers, men who were approximately twenty years older than he was, and drove trucks or minivans, and were married, and rarely, if ever, smoked pot, or for that matter, listened to Lynyrd Skynyrd.

I think both of us felt out of place at the father-and-son campout. After all, we had only met once before, when Matt had come over to the house to change the lightbulbs on the front and back porch.

"Hey, little man," he said to me, looking down from his ladder, "how can I put a bulb in this thing when there's already a bulb in it? Do you know what I mean, dude?"

On the last night of the campout, we were sitting around a fire and the fathers were telling about their favorite memory with their sons, and when it came time for Matt to talk about me he sat silent for a minute. As I said, Matt and I had spent little time together before the campout. I was searching my mind for any kind of memory, and considered talking about that great time he changed the lightbulbs, how he had to move the ladder a couple times, and how I helped him by turning the switch on and off. I knew it was a boring story, but I thought I might embellish it a bit by insisting both of us got electrocuted and had to give each other CPR. But then Matt broke the silence. Having searched for any kind of memory himself, he told about the car ride on the way *to* the campout: how we stopped at McDonalds and had to jumpstart the bug, and how we played air guitar and bashed our heads against the dashboard to the tune of "Sweet Home Alabama."

"Times with our sons, or with our neighbors' kids are important, do you know what I mean, dude?" Matt said to the fathers, most of them looking very confused. I nodded my head.

"I know what you mean," I said, breaking the awkward silence.

"Sure you do, Doug," he chortled, rubbing my head.

"Don," I corrected. "My name is Don."

"Sure it is, little man," he said to me with a confused look on his face.

Then Matt, realizing his story had fallen flat, started telling us how he made out with a cheerleader in the janitor's closet when he was in high school. Another father stopped him just short of second base. A prepubescent, collective grunt went out when the story was interrupted, but Matt finished it the next day when we were waiting in line to get in a canoe. The smell of ammonia, apparently, still turned him on.

———

MATT WAS GREAT, but not much of a guide in the father-sense. And he went off to the army shortly after the camp-out, so I never learned important things he knew like how to actually *get* the girl to go *into* the janitor's closet or how to drive for two years without a license.

The next guy was more fatherly but straight as an arrow, which was nice for a change, but he was also nuts. His name was Mr. Kilpin and he went to our church. His thing was to fly remote-control airplanes in a field. It was exciting at first, for about twenty minutes or so, but he would never let me control the plane. He would stand there wearing some sort of military hat he must have picked up in Vietnam, and his eyes would get big as planets as he made the plane dip down and sweep across the field, all the while making bombing noises with his mouth.

"Did you see that, Donald?" he'd ask. "You got those commie bastards," I'd say, sort of looking around for a Frisbee or something. I kept asking, every two minutes, if he would let me fly the plane, but each time he would say maybe next time, maybe just for a few seconds the next time we went out. I had to endure three weekends of simulated bombing runs over the Mekong Delta before he finally gave in to my pestering and let me take the sticks. Within eight seconds I had flown the thing into a tree, at which point Mr. Kilpin shrieked and ran across the field, shouting, "We've got men down, we've got men on the ground!"

All the way home he lectured me about the kinds of torture a captured pilot has to endure, and we never spent any time together after that.

———

THE NEXT GUY was an enormous improvement, and proved to be just what I needed as a makeshift father figure. He was the youth minister at my church and was hired about the time I started junior high. His name was David Gentiles, and because most last names are derived from what our ancestors did for a living, I assumed David had come from a small community that politely wanted to differentiate themselves from Jews. David could never authenticate my suspicion, but I told him this was probably the case. I lived about three blocks from the church, so I would go over and visit David in his office. I sat across from him, talking about the state of affairs in the world, football, the weather, girls, all the while going through his desk looking for rubber bands I could shoot at him while he tried to study the Bible. I'd find pencils I could fling into the ceiling tiles, or explain, at length, the many ways he could rearrange his office. David never asked me to leave, and looking back I have no idea why. Either he enjoyed being around me, or he was a good actor. Regardless, he liked my ideas and would nod in agreement when I told him he didn't need a desk, that Ronald Reagan worked standing up, and this would free space in his office for a small putting green and a contraption that shoots the golf ball back to you.

I used to sit and look at the books on David's shelf, asking intelligent and probing questions about each one.

What's that book about the Civil War about? I'd say.

The Civil War, he'd answer.

What about that one about Abraham Lincoln?

That one's just a cookbook, he'd tell me.

After I inquired about twenty or so of his books, he asked if I was interested in books. I told him I didn't know anything about them, that the problem with most books is they were too long. Then he turned me on to some poetry, which was good because it was shorter. David said girls just loved the stuff. I went home and read through a lot of it and memorized a couple, and he seemed pretty impressed with that. He asked me, a little later, if I had ever thought about writing. He told me he thought I had a knack for understanding poetry and wondered if I would be interested in writing a guest editorial for the youth group newsletter.

"I've seen a lot of growth in you, Don," he said while we were walking down the church hallway. "You've really got a way with words, and your spiritual life has developed uniquely, quite beautifully, and I feel like you could deal with spirituality in a delicate manner, getting to the heart of our faith. Would you be interested in writing an article?"

"Does the Pope crap in the woods?" I told him.

I spent the next week poring over the dictionary for the biggest, most obscure words I could find—words like loquacious and flabbergasted. I was going to knock Dave's socks off with my smarts. The first sentence of my article read:

"The loquaciousness of pious rhetoric has developed into a pariah in the corridors of First Baptist Church."

The article was about how everybody was stupid except for me and Dave, and went on to name the top ten most boring people at First Baptist Church.

I turned the article in to David and he sat behind his desk and kind of hummed and coughed as he read, his eyes getting big and his hands flattening the paper and his head suddenly jolting back when he came to the end of a paragraph. He put his hand on his forehead and looked at me in bewilderment, probably wondering how such brilliant writing could come at such a young age. "Good use of exclamation points," he finally said. "Your punctuation is remarkable."

And looking back, I believe it was. I've always been good at punctuation!

David kindly explained, however, the article might be a bit critical, and I might consider writing about something I like—people I like, perhaps—or do a review of a movie or a record, or maybe write up a concert or something going on at school. I told him those were all good ideas, but as a journalist, I would need to make up my own mind about what I would write and that, as much as I respected him, I wasn't going to be a pawn of The Man.

"Would never ask you to compromise," David said.

"Thanks," I told him, leaning back in my chair and crossing my legs. "I am not a fan of corporate."

"Me neither," he said with a confused look on his face.

There happened to be a talent show going on at school that week, and I decided I would interview some of the talent and write a review. I sat in the back with a notebook on my lap, hoping people would ask why I had that notebook on my lap, or for that matter a pencil behind each ear, or for that matter a hat with an index card on which was printed the word PRESS. I roamed during the show, walking the aisles, trying to get a feel for audience reaction. Then I went backstage as a band called *Dead Man Sweat* did a partially intelligible, twelve-minute rendition of "Pour Some Sugar on Me," toward the end of which the lead singer opened a bag of sugar and poured it over his long, dark hair, causing the principal to put an end to the music. The lead singer had to sweep up the mess before three girls came out and did a dance from the movie *Flashdance*. The girls danced sultrily against and on top of chairs as some guys from the football team squirted water on them from the wings. This was also, unfortunately, interrupted. But I interviewed them all. I interviewed the rock band, asking, "Sugar is a metaphor for what?" Earlier that week, I had learned what a metaphor was, and the concept fascinated me. "Leg warmers are a metaphor for what?" I asked the girls who did the *Flashdance.*

Then this girl came up, this girl from my youth group, whom I had mostly ignored that year, and she stepped to the microphone and shyly said, "Hello," and that she would like to sing a Christian song for Jesus. I dropped my pencil. It's social suicide, I thought. You can't sing a song for Jesus at a high school talent show. The audience threw out some cold remarks about going back to Mayberry, and when the piano accompaniment started, she belted out quite possibly the worst rendition of "His Eye Is on the Sparrow" ever performed, save Roger Bobo's tuba rendition with the Canadian Brass.

The crowd had a field day. It was like *The Gong Show.* People were rolling in the aisles. And standing backstage I started feeling a little sorry for her, and then something strange happened in my chest. What I mean is, there is this fight or flight thing that happens when you decide whether you were going to associate with — or disassociate yourself from — somebody who has fallen down or coughed up their food, whether you were going to say you never knew her, didn't attend the same church, didn't worship the same God, or whether you were going to, well, clap. And I clapped. I mean when she finished, I clapped, and I meant it. It felt good to take a stand for somebody who nobody else was taking a stand for. And she came off the stage and I asked her what the sparrow was a metaphor for, and then I told her I thought she did a great job, that I was proud of her. She looked at me with this huge smile and you could tell she was very nervous and relieved at the same time. And I went home that night and wrote an article saying I thought God might have been kind of happy with the talent show, and I wrote about how I thought we should all be willing to make complete idiots of ourselves for God, and how even if our voices sound like *a chicken in a cage with a ferret*, we should be willing to praise God with the pipes God gave us. The tag line at the end of the article, the real clincher, the tearjerker exclamation point was this:

And even though everybody in the auditorium was booing that night, and even though Monica shouldn't be allowed to sing the national anthem at a chess tournament, the angels in heaven were clapping, and the opinions of angels matter more than the opinions of people, because angels can fly.

I gave the article to Monica first, and I stood there while she read it, and about halfway through her eyes started to water, and about three-fourths through she put her hand over her mouth, and when she finished she looked me in the eye with the tenderest, most vulnerable look, dropped the piece of paper, and ran down the hall of the math wing. I knew then that I had the gift—that David Gentiles was right, that I could move people with words, encourage them and change their lives forever. And even though Dave thought it best I rewrite the article and take out several of the harsher adjectives and the bit about the *chicken in a cage with a ferret*, the thing still had power. I got a lot of calls from people at the church, and people stopped me in the halls to say *good job*, and *that line about angels having wings was an interesting point.*

I only tell you this to say David Gentiles, who could have done just about anything else with his time, decided to spend time with me and give me a shot at writing. He was somebody who stepped into my life and helped me believe I was here on purpose, and for a purpose. I don't think there are very many things more important than this when we are kids.

The truth I've learned about life is you can't do it on your own. People don't do well independently. One generation passes wisdom to the next, wisdom about girls and faith and punctuation. And we won't be as good a person if we don't receive it.

And in life, I figure, you are going to pretty much do the things that make you feel good about yourself, make you feel important and on purpose, and walk away from the things that make you feel like a loser. I distinctly remember this phase in my life, this time when I started writing, as a kind of fork in the road. On one hand, a good friend and I had just discovered a quick and easy way to break into houses, stealing loose change from jars on people's dressers. And then there was this church thing going on, and it wasn't like I was deciding which person I was going to become; it's more like I was swimming in a river and there were two equal currents. I could have very easily ended up in prison—first breaking into houses, then falling in with the wrong crowd, then drugs, and so on and so on. A statistic. David Gentiles was the person who threw out a rope. He was a father figure. People assume when you're swimming in a river you are supposed to know which way you are going, and I guess some of the time that is true, but there are certain currents that are very strong, and it's when we are in those currents we need somebody to come along, pull us out, and guide us in a safer direction.

Chapter Two

OUR PROBLEM:
TO OWN A DRAGON

All my life I have been fascinated by stuff that isn't there. I'd be lying to you if I said I read books early. I didn't start reading till I was in college, but I knew about fairies and dragons and trolls from hearing about them at reading time when the librarian at my elementary school crossed her long legs and sat silently until we sat silently. Then she'd wrap her lips around the simple words of a children's book, holding her palm against the crease of the page, turning the book toward us to display the watercolor pictures—a small troll in a big coat who lived under a bridge, his eye ever alert for travelers on the road. There was a book with pictures of a boy riding a dragon through the clouds, smoke and fire coming from the creature's nostrils, the boy leaning in as the dragon ascended over a pleasant village. And I remember wondering what it would be like to own a dragon, to lie across the monster's spine, inching toward its neck as the beast jolted into flight, thrusting through the milky pretext for heaven that glows over Houston, up and above the weather where my dragon and I could watch lightning fight itself into exhaustion.

I bring this up because in writing some thoughts about a father, or not having a father, I feel as though I am writing a book about a dragon or a troll under a bridge. For me a father is nothing more than a character in a fairy tale. And I know fathers are not like dragons in that fathers actually exist, but I don't remember feeling that a father existed for me. I know they are real people. I have seen them on television, and sliding their arms around their women in grocery stores, and I have seen them in the malls and in the coffee shops, but these were characters in other people's stories, and I never stopped to question why one of these characters wasn't living in our house. I don't say this out of self-pity, because in a way I don't miss having a father any more than I miss having a dragon. But in another way, I find myself wondering if I missed out on something important.

What I mean is that by design, within the laws of nature, a man and a woman join and make kids, and at least you would assume the father is supposed to stick around and teach his kids to carve a turkey at Thanksgiving or whatever it is a father teaches a kid. But, that never happened to me, and if you are reading this book it may have never happened to you, either.

It makes you wonder if just having a dad around—just his being there reading the morning paper and smoking cigars at poker with his friends and having him read you a story at night—you were supposed to understand something, some idea God in heaven wanted to offer as a gift. Lately, I have been curious about what that something is, and whether or not a person could understand it even if his father took off.

———

I LEARNED A great deal about myself while watching a documentary a few years ago about elephants in a wildlife trust in Africa. There were twenty-five elephants, all of them orphans, and they had been brought to the trust twenty years before. They were becoming teenagers—in elephant years. The girls were adequate, getting along with the other elephants, but there were a few boys who were causing a great deal of trouble. The narrator talked about the frustrations these few elephants were feeling because they had gone into early musth cycles, which showed up as a green pus running down their right hind leg. This phase produced aggressive and violent behavior, the elephant equivalent of sexual frustration.

The narrator in the documentary said the elephant musth

cycle begins in adolescence, and normally lasts only a few days. But among these orphans, the musth cycle was disrupted and had become unusually long. These elephants were taking out their aggression on rhinos that bathed at a local mud pool. An elephant would slowly lumber down to the pool, enter near a rhino, then spear it through the side with his tusks. The elephant would then lean his gargantuan forehead into the head of the rhino, holding the beast underwater until it drowned. The filmmakers followed these orphan elephants, who were always on their own, staggering about the wildlife refuge, fueled by a pent-up aggression they couldn't under-stand. They weren't acting like elephants—they didn't know what an elephant was supposed to do with all his energy, all his muscle.

Occasionally, two elephants in musth would meet, and the encounter was always violent, going so far as to uproot trees in the fray of their brawl. When both beasts, bloodied, lumbered their separate ways alone—without a family, without a tribe—I couldn't help but identify. I have never killed a rhino, or much of anything for that matter, but there have been times in my life when I didn't know exactly how to be. I mean, there were feelings, sometimes anger, sometimes depression, sometimes raging lust, and I was never sure what any of it was about. I just felt like killing some-body, or sleeping with some girl, or decking a guy in a bar, and I didn't know what to do with any of these feelings. Life was a confusing series of emotions rubbing against events.

I wasn't sure how to manage myself, how to talk to a woman, how to build a career, how to—well, be a man.

To me, life was something you had to stumble through alone. It wasn't something you enjoyed or conquered, it was something that happened to you, and you didn't have a whole lot of say about the way it turned out. You just acted out your feelings and hoped you'd never get caught.

Watching television that night, however, the narrator began to speak of a kind of hope for these elephants. Elephant development, apparently, begins very early. Female elephants are only capable of having children once every two years, and during those two years between babies, the young are cared for obsessively by their mothers. They are fed, sheltered, loved, and guided in their learning of basic survival.

It is only at the first musth cycle that a young male elephant leaves his mother and enters into the African wild, searching for a mentor, a guide. The green pus running down his hind leg and his smell like fresh-cut grass alerts an older, fully mature male, that this is a young elephant in need of guidance. Upon finding a mentor, the young elephant's musth cycle ends. The older and younger begin to travel together, to find food together, to protect each other—the older one teaching the younger what elephant strength is for, and how to use it for the benefit of himself and the tribe.

Watching television that night, I wondered if humans

aren't like that, too. I began to wonder if we guys weren't designed to have a father, whose very presence would cause us to understand more accurately what our muscle is for, what we are supposed to do with our energy.

You have to wonder, don't you? Some statistics state as many as 85 percent of the guys in prison grew up without a dad. This is sobering to me.

And so watching the documentary, I began to wonder if those of us without dads aren't making mistakes in our lives we wouldn't make if we had a father to guide us. I wondered if there isn't a better paradigm for our existence—a way of being men, a way each of us could truly embrace if it were instilled in us by a man who spoke with altruism and authority. I wondered if people who grow up with great fathers don't walk around with a subconscious sense they are wanted on this planet, that they belong, and the world needs them. And I wondered this: Is there practical information we are supposed to know about work, women, decisions, authority, leadership, marriage, and family that we would have learned if there were a guide around to help us navigate our journey? I wondered if some of the confusing emotions I was feeling weren't a kind of suspended adolescence from which the presence of an older man might have delivered me.

Chapter Three

THE MENTOR:
TERRI SAID I COULD MAKE A SANDWICH

The truth is, I'd rather do things my way. I thought the confusion I felt growing up without a father was just part of life, and there seemed to be benefits. Life was an open range. I disliked authority figures, because they represented boundaries. And the worst were older men. For reasons I didn't understand, I resented them. I felt as though they wanted me to submit to their authority because they wanted to feel powerful. But I also wanted their respect and approval. And if I sensed disapproval, I belittled them in my mind. I was a split person: Half of me wanted to be mentored through life—the side, I suppose, who wanted a father—and the other half would rather not answer to anybody. I started realizing this several years ago when I moved in with a family, the family of a man who taught a college class at a church I was attending.

I met John MacMurray at a strange time in my life. I had left my home in Houston and was traveling around the country when I ran out of money in Oregon. I got an apartment in the suburbs of Portland where housing was cheap, and I started going to a church in a town called Boring, Oregon. The town lived up to its name. It had one stoplight, a convenience store, and a burger place. It was very beautiful, mind you, with views of Mount Hood and Mount St. Helens, river valleys and all, but once you were over that stuff, you were out of luck. The church I started attending was in the middle of a shrub farm—landscape shrubs and flowers and Christmas trees. Every November, the Christmas trees would be hauled down to schmucks in Florida who paid fifty bucks to hang lights on them, sing some songs, then watch them dry up and get pine tar all over the wicker furniture. This church was crowded with tree farmers, hunters, fishermen, that sort of thing— men's men.

I was born going to church, raised going to church, and church had been a significant part of my life. I confess it's been comforting to me, at dark times, to know there is a God in the cosmos who is paying attention. I had walked away from a lot of it, but when I moved to Oregon, I was feeling lonely so I decided to plug back in to a church. They had a college group that met at a guy's house way out in the sticks, this guy I was telling you about, and I started driving out there once a week.

At first, I didn't know what to think of the group. Or of John MacMurray, the guy who led it. We would sit around in his big living room, on the floor, because even though he seemed to have money, he was too cheap to buy his wife furniture. After we made small talk for a while, John would sit down in a chair, the only chair in the room, and everybody would get quiet. The place fell to a hush. This took me a while to get used to, and I don't mean to make the guy sound like a strange guru or something—it's just that when he sat down in the chair, everybody shut up, waiting for him to speak. And the first thing John would say is, "What do you guys want to talk about?" He wasn't being weird or anything, and these people really respected the guy, so I paid attention. The hush made me wonder what kind of guy I was dealing with, and I half expected him to lay his Bible across his lap, press his palms together, nod slowly, and say something like, "In order for us to become great, we must make ourselves small"—and everybody would respond with a worshipful sigh, to which I would have laughed out loud. Thank heavens, nothing like this happened. He turned out to be pretty normal, and the hush that came over the group was mostly because people didn't want to miss anything. This guy was that smart. Basically, apart from retreats where all we did was play Scrabble or cards and watch movies, the church's college program involved sitting around with John leading us in studying and talking about the Bible.

The other thing you have to know about John is that, at first, he can come off a bit cocky. It's not a bad cocky—in fact, it's quite endearing sometimes, once you get used to it. Partly, he has this personality trait because he grew up in Philadelphia, and roughly everybody from Philadelphia sounds like they think they are better than you. It's true. Panhandlers on the street sound condescending in Philadelphia. Anyway, we all grew to like it. Sometimes you get tired of people kissing your butt all the time, and you just wish someone would speak their mind. That's John.

Now, I don't know where you are spiritually, whether you are a Muslim or a Jew or an agnostic or just prefer not to think about it, but there is something good about listening to somebody explain complicated ideas, especially when they have to do with ancient themes—meaning-of-life themes—because listening to that stuff gives you the feeling life is a great deal more intricate, and perhaps more beautiful, than you thought. Studying an ancient text makes a person feel as though they are living in a complicated but wondrous reality that is greater than they are.

John was a Bible scholar, but he didn't teach the Bible for a living. He had a part-time gig teaching at a local school, but for a living, he took landscape photographs. I found this out because some of us would stay around after the Bible study and watch whatever was on television, and one time I asked John about the photographs he and his wife had hanging in the living room. They had landscape photographs, mountains and snow and sunsets and the like, a couple of them on the walls and one of them over the fireplace. These weren't normal nature photographs, like the ones your uncle took of the family in front of a waterfall in Kentucky, but the real thing, almost like art. These were the sorts of photographs you took by being dropped off by helicopter on a mountaintop just at sunrise, no footprints or anything. And that's when John told me they were his. I didn't believe him at first, but he shook his head and shrugged his shoulders like it didn't matter whether I believed him or not. That's when I started thinking maybe he was telling the truth.

Even though John is too cheap to buy his wife furniture, they live in a nice house. It sprawls out on a couple acres, and from the driveway you look directly at Mount Hood, all eleven thousand feet of purple-on-snow rising out of the rolling hills of western Oregon. I always wondered, when I went out to John's house, how he could afford a big place like that on a Bible teacher's salary, especially only teaching one class a year. It started making sense that he might have some kind of side job.

We would hang out after Bible study, sitting in the den watching Sports Center, and one evening John asked if I wanted to see some of his work. The rest of the guys got quiet. Sure, whatever, I said. The others stood up, and John looked at them with this kind of Bruce Willis glance and said, "I guess you guys want to see, too."

We went upstairs to John's office—a kind of library without shelves. There were stacks of black boxes all over the floor and on the desk, and John led us meandering through them. He flipped a switch on his desk and half the thing lit up—not a top light, but the actual desk was made of glass and it lit from underneath. John opened one of the black boxes and set down a couple slides on the backlit desk. These slides were pretty big, four inches by five, John told me, and when they were lit from behind they were remarkable. I couldn't believe a guy could get paid to go to the most beautiful places in the world to take pictures.

John would tell us what they were—one a mountaintop in Italy, the next the Coral Reef in Australia, then a waterfall in the Jefferson Wilderness here in Oregon. He must have had more than a hundred slides in each box, and there were hundreds of boxes. All the guys stood around the light board like we were looking at pictures of naked ladies, because we were honestly amazed, none of us able to take it all in—the perfection of the colors and the textures, moonlight reflecting on a glacier with a gray mountain peak in silhouette rising up in the background, a single flower in a meadow along a creek banked with green moss, pines so thick with snow you could hardly see the green within the pure white pillows that piled along their laboring branches, water surging over a five-hundred-foot cliff to a blue pool below, the water seeming to move in the still photo.

There were times we would meet at John's house and somebody would substitute teach, and John would come back the next week with another stack of slides—fall colors on the Blue Ridge Parkway, winter in a Scottish glen, the Swiss Alps, ranges in New Zealand you hardly believed were real. I asked him why he didn't put his name in huge letters at the bottom of his photos and make a fortune off posters at tourist shops in Yosemite Park or somewhere. But he rolled his eyes. I'm serious, I said, you could get some serious cash out of this stuff.

"I do fine," John said.

"I'm just saying," I told him.

I got to feeling pretty comfortable around the MacMurrays. After a while, you don't notice that whole Philadelphia thing, and it hardly mattered because we were learning the Bible inside and out. I even started going over there when there wasn't a Bible study. Terri, John's wife, would invite me out for Saturday breakfast, and then we'd all sit and watch golf or talk about John's last trip. They had this little boy named Chris, who was cute as a puppy, and it didn't hurt that Terri looked like a supermodel, either. John would make eyes at her while she chased Chris around the island in the kitchen. I liked being with them and was kind of honored that good-looking, rich people would want me hanging around.

One night after Bible study, I was feeling pretty hungry

because I hadn't eaten any dinner. I went to the kitchen, and Terri said I could make myself a sandwich. I'm not the type to go rummaging around in somebody else's fridge without permission, but Terri said I could. And there I was all aglow in the light of the refrigerator when John walked into the kitchen.

"Well, make yourself at home, Miller," he said to me.

"Terri said I could make a sandwich."

"Feel like you live here, don't you, Miller?"

"Terri said I could make a sandwich."

"Well, you might as well move in if you're going to eat all our food," John said to me, smiling. "You can pick up the key from Terri. The apartment is above the garage." And with that, he walked back into the living room. I got a plate out of the cupboard and was opening a loaf of bread when Terri walked through the swinging door from the living room.

"It will be great to have another man around," she said. "I always have to lift those bags of pellets for the wood stove when John is out taking pictures, but you can do that. I'll get you a key."

"A key to what?" I asked.

"The apartment is above the garage," she said, and pulled a key out of the junk drawer. "You should just do what John tells you. It's easier that way," she said, handing me the key.

"You guys really want me to move in?" I asked.

"Guess so," she said with a smile.

So that is how I moved in with John and Terri. And that is also how, without knowing it, I suddenly had an authority figure in my life. John is not the kind of guy who wants you living upstairs at his house if he doesn't want to teach you something. I didn't know that when he invited me, otherwise I wouldn't have moved in, but it was true. I lived with him and Terri for four years, and I was there when the next two kids were born, Elle and Cassy. And I was there when they got a dog, and I always took the Christmas picture, and I overheard John and Terri fight, and I—more than once—had to go back to my apartment when they were cuddling a little too intimately.

What I am trying to say is, I saw a family. For the first time in my life, I saw what a father does, what a father teaches a kid, what a husband does around the house, the way a man interacts with the world around him, the way a man—just as does a woman—holds a family together.

I am not going to tell you it was easy. There were times I would have rather lived on my own, played my music as loud as I wanted, come home drunk, whatever. But playing your music as loud as you want and coming home drunk aren't real life. Real life, it turns out, is diapers and lawnmowers, decks that need painting, a wife that needs to be listened to, kids that need to be taught right from wrong, a checkbook, an oil change, a sunset behind a mountain, laughter at a kitchen table, too much wine, a chipped tooth, and a screaming child. The lessons I learned in the four years

I spent with John and Terri will stay with me forever.

I read a passage in the Bible a long time ago that said, "God sets the lonely in families." Looking back on the time with John and Terri, I know that passage was talking about me.

Chapter Four

BELONGING:
WHAT THE EISENHOWERS KNEW

The first thing you will notice when you move in with a healthy family is that they cannot work independently. In the first place, there is too much labor involved in raising kids for anybody to sit on the couch for an extended period of time. They are a unit, like a body with different organs, or a car with different working parts. Both John and Terri provided incomes. Terri had a great job at an insurance agency downtown, and didn't want to leave because they wanted the health benefits. They liked her so much she worked from home most days, but still she worked. John watched the kids when Terri was busy or running errands in town, and Terri looked after everything when John was on a trip. But it wasn't just the adults who had important roles. In a way, so did the kids. It was obvious, watching them and being around them, that John and Terri took great delight in their children. They were better than television to them. And the kids felt important, I think, because they would do silly things to make their parents laugh, or dangerous things and have them screaming or talking them down off the balcony railing.

It all reminded me of a book I read a few years ago called *At Ease: Stories I Tell to Friends*. It was written by Dwight D. Eisenhower, the World War II general who became president. I've always been curious about very successful men, leaders, and what they know the rest of us don't. This book was entertaining, because Eisenhower was a character, getting himself kicked out of West Point, causing a lot of trouble. But always there was in him a sense of confidence, a sense he would become somebody important. And more than this, he believed the world *needed* him — that if he didn't exist, things would fall apart. He believed he was called to be a great man. I wondered, as I read, where he got this confidence, and that's when Eisenhower started talking about his family, about how his mother had the New Testament memorized and was always giving her kids wisdom from what she knew.

Then Eisenhower said something I thought was incredible, so incredible I had to close the book and sit and think about the ramifications.

Dwight Eisenhower said his mother and father made an assumption that set the course of his life—*that the world could be fixed of its problems if every child understood the necessity of their existence.* Eisenhower's parents assumed if their children weren't alive, their family couldn't function.

I found this striking, and I wondered what it would have been like if, as a kid, I had felt completely needed by my family. My mother needed me, it is true, and she was certainly loving, but she was also burdened with paying bills, working late, and managing life as a single parent. For the better part of my childhood, at least on weekdays, my sister and I were left alone. Weekends would have my mother home, and we would take outings, fly kites, go to children's museums and plays. But even this was more stimulation and entertainment for us than it was rest for her. She mothered herself into exhaustion. Weekdays, Mom would work late, often coming home right around our bedtime, and even then we were all too tired to act like a family. I knew, somehow, that my mother's long working hours were because of my sister and me. But I never thought to ascribe my mother's emotional and physical exhaustion to the lack of a husband and father; rather, I ascribed it to my existence. There were times, I confess, I wondered whether my family would be better off without me. I grew up believing that if I had never been born, things would be easier for the people I loved.

A thought like this can cripple a kid for a long time. This may sound like so much psychobabble, but to me it's become an obvious truth. If a kid grows up feeling he is burdening the people around him, he is going to operate as though the world doesn't want him. I didn't recognize this feeling in myself until the last few years—into my late twenties and early thirties—but it has always been there. Because of this, I notice I pull out of a conversation when it gets too personal. And despite the strongest of invitations to connect, I feel, intrinsically, that the other person will eventually be burdened by his or her relationship with me. I find myself doing a great job at small talk, trying to be charming and all, but when it comes time for a person to actually know me, I run for the hills. Any ability I have to be charming also comes from this desire not to be a burden. If I am light and easy to be around, my community won't want to throw me out, or they won't meditate at night on what a wonderful world theirs would be if I were not involved.

So, it struck me as I read Eisenhower that my self-understanding is the binary opposite of his self-understanding. It's no wonder he grew up to become president. If you believe your family will fall apart without you, you probably go on to believe your community will fall apart without you, and then your city and country. And in just about every dynamic you walk into, you would feel the need to lead, to hold things together, to bring life and service to the people you interact with—just as you had done when you were a kid with your family

And conversely, you can't blame a kid for feeling

unwanted if his father takes off. If you think about it, God gives a father a specific instinct that makes him love his kid more than anything in the world. And I suppose that same instinct was floating around in my father's brain, too, but for whatever reason, he took a look at me and split. Even the instinct God gave him wasn't strong enough to make my dad stay. And that has made me feel, at times, there is this detestable person living within my skin who makes people feel as though they must carry me on their backs. Walking through the park one night I realized I was operating out of a feeling of inferiority. Deep inside, I believed life was for other people—that joy was for others, and responsibility was for others, and so on and so on. In life, there were people who were meant to live and people who were accidentally born, elected to plod the globe as the despised.

These thoughts are illogical, I realize. There isn't any proof that a guy who grows up in a family with a good dad is any better than a guy who grows up in a family with a bad one. Still, a logical argument isn't able to change the heart. My mind knew there was nothing wrong with me—that the problem was the message my father handed down—but this *knowledge* didn't make me *feel* any more secure. For many years, all I could do in the healing process was recognize I felt inferior and tell myself this feeling was a lie. For a long time, I couldn't go any further than this.

The continents began to shift during this time with John and Terri. There were times I would watch John interact with

Chris and I would get jealous. I'm not saying I was jealous of *Chris*, and I don't even know if jealousy is the word I am looking for. I only mean I would feel a sense of unfairness. The idea that *I* mattered had not been instilled in me the way John was instilling it in Chris. Chris will never have to learn he matters, or at least he will not have to swim up a stream of lies.

The MacMurray family dynamics allowed me to picture what should have existed in my own life. It's not that I wanted John to pick me up and set me on his lap. But it did make me wonder why God would allow me to grow up without a father saying he loved me or was glad I was around.

It's odd to be talking about this as an adult. But as I've begun to process the consequences of growing up without a father, I've realized the incredible hole in my heart this absence has left. I wish my father and I had a friendship, and that he would call once every couple weeks and tell me I was doing a good job. I hunger for this. I don't actually like thinking about this stuff, but I have a sense that wounds don't heal until you feel them. What I mean is, I could lash out against the world for the rest of my life and never stop to do the hard work of asking why I am angry or why I feel pain, then come to the difficult truth that the pain is there because I wanted to be loved, and I wasn't. I wanted to be important to my father, but I wasn't. I wanted to be guided, but I wasn't. And then, honestly, to feel whatever it is that hard truth creates — to respond in the way I needed to respond.

Not long ago these truths came crashing into my emotions. It was the week before Father's Day, and a few of my friends had told me they were planning large dinners or trips to be with their dads. Perhaps it was because I was operating on so little sleep following a trip I had taken — or perhaps it was because Father's Day is a foreign concept to me, like celebrating relationships with aliens — but on a particular night, I felt my soul collapsing. I was struggling against a writing deadline and feeling, as I often do, that whatever book I wrote would only hit the world as a burden to its library. I wanted a father to walk through the door and tell me this wasn't true, that I was here on purpose, and I had a purpose, and that a family and a father and even a world needed me to exist to make himself and themselves more happy. And it occurred to me, then, that a father was not going to walk through the door, that there would be no encouragement, there would be no voice of calm, there would be no larger, mature elephant whose presence would correct the stray thoughts in my mind. It occurred to me this would never, ever happen. For the first time in my life, I realized, deep down, I never had a dad.

I don't cry much, but on that night I did. I lost it. I shoved my computer aside and buried my head in my pillow like a child and sobbed. I sobbed for nearly an hour. I hate saying this because it sounds so weak, and I don't like dramatics, but

I remember the night quite well, and there was no question something busted open.

Somebody said that realizing we are broken is the beginning of healing. And for me, some of the healing began that night.

Because my mom made us go to church when we were kids, I have always been a person who prays. I don't understand why, but I have never had much of a problem talking to God. I haven't always liked reading the Bible or going to church, but I think from an early age God kicked open the door to His office and made sure I knew I could barge in at any time. When I started feeling a lot of self-pity about not having a father — when I realized the stuff going on at the MacMurray house had never happened at my house — I started asking God why. I don't like saying this, but my attitude at first was quite accusatory; that is, I went to God saying, *You shafted me. Why didn't I get a father to tell me he loved me, to teach me all this stuff?*

I don't think God got offended when I accused Him; I think He was understanding. Praying those honest prayers led to a series of epiphanies that helped a great deal. Watching John interact with Chris, I realized what I really wanted, what my soul was longing for, was *belonging.* By that I mean I wanted a father to take ownership of me, to care about me more than he cared about anything else in the world, or, for that matter, *anybody* else in the world. And it was something John told me after a hair-raising drive to

Lost Lake that made me believe, even though I didn't have a father, this idea was still true for me.

———

I WAS WASHING my car one afternoon when John came out and invited me to go with him to Lost Lake, deep in the Cascade Wilderness. He wanted to shoot a view of Mount Hood from the north. On the drive up, John told a story about the last time he had been to Lost Lake. He had navigated the thin forest service roads on a snowmobile, hoping to photograph the snow on the pines around the banks of the lake and the white cathedral of a mountain reflected in the water.

"No kidding," John said, telling me the story, a cup of lemonade in his free hand and the other gripping the steering wheel, cornering the back country bends about ten miles-per-hour too fast. "It probably took four hours to get up there. I mean, we've been driving for an hour or more, right, and we've still got half an hour to go."

Waving his cup at the landscape beyond the windshield, John said, "Imagine all of this covered in snow — how long it would take on a snowmobile." He took a drink of his lemonade and turned his head behind him to see if there was any color on the mountain. I could hardly keep myself from reaching over to grab the steering wheel as John slid off the road, pulled the truck back onto the shoulder, and then, without so much as lifting his foot off the gas pedal, turned around again to check the color on the mountain.

"Did you get your shot?" I questioned, squinting and grimacing as seven-hundred-year-old trees blurred by only inches from the mirror outside my door.

"Well," John continued, still looking back at the mountain, "I got up there and, of course, the sky was thick with clouds. Nothing. I mean you could see the mountain, but the west was all low clouds and there was no color, nothing to shoot at all. I couldn't believe it, because I was freezing and I had rented this snowmobile, and I was getting pretty frustrated. I kept checking my watch, knowing there were only a few minutes left before sunset."

"And you still had to drive the snowmobile back to the road," I said.

"Exactly. I had another three or four hours to get back, this time in the dark." John shook his head and rolled his eyes as the truck slipped off the road again. He jerked it back while taking a sip of his lemonade.

"No shot, right?" I questioned again, slyly slipping on my seat belt.

"Well," John continued, "I started packing up my gear. I had the camera wrapped up and put away in my bag and was taking down the tripod when, out of nowhere, here comes this shaft of orange light, like at a rock concert." John pointed out the front window as if toward the mountain as he spoke. "I'm telling you," he said, "this incredible light was shining out like heaven split open, all the rays flooding Ladd Glacier, the color mirrored perfectly in the still lake, the snow in the pines all aglow—the whole bit, right? It was like magic or something."

"And you had put your camera away."

"I had put my camera away. Yeah. But I got it out." At this point, John looked right into my eyes, not paying attention to the road. I kept looking out the front window, gripping the dashboard with my fingernails, wondering at what point we were going to drive off a cliff. John must have thought his truck had auto-pilot, I reasoned, trying to rationalize his insane driving. He took a breath and kept talking, still not looking at the road. He even took his hands off the wheel to motion how, exactly, he unwrapped his camera. Terror was taking over my bodily functions.

"So I unwrapped it, bolted it to the tripod, inserted the film." John started motioning like he was putting film into his camera. I started gasping a little, my fingernails moving from the dashboard to the armrest, my other hand clutching the seat belt, my eyes feeling like they were crawling back into my head. "Then I focused," he continued, turning his hand like he was turning a knob, "and hit the button." As John said this, he clenched his hand into a fist and tapped his thumb against the other fingers, like a guy with a grenade. He then reached down and picked up his lemonade, put his hand back on the wheel, and steered left no more than two feet from a giant evergreen. I audibly gasped as the branches of the tree scraped the side of the truck. I slipped down into the seat and stared up at the ceiling, breathing out a kind of thanks to God for letting me live through the near miss of the tree, not to mention the cliff a mile back.

"Exactly," John said, shaking his head, responding to my gasp. "I almost didn't get the shot!"

"What shot?" I said, looking at him as though he were crazy.

"The one of Mount Hood. Haven't you been listening?" John shook his head.

"I was listening," I lied, sliding deeper into my seat.

"I am telling you," he continued, "as soon as I hit that button, the color started to fade, and within a minute, it was all gone. I couldn't believe it. God showed up on that one, for sure."

I slid back up in my seat, hoping John wouldn't launch into another story and forget he had a truck to drive. I composed myself and adjusted the air conditioning vents.

"So you think God did that?" I asked, feeling a bit more comfortable as the road straightened out and started climbing again.

"Do I think God did what? The sunset?" John clarified.

"Yeah, the sunset."

"No, Don. I don't think God did it." My friend shook his head again. "I think Mother Teresa did it."

"Very funny," I said.

"Of course He did it. Who else would have done it? Spielberg? Hiding in the trees with some lasers? It was God!"

"He did it just so you could see it. Just so you could take the shot?" I questioned, the doubt in my voice coming through clearly.

"Well, no, I mean I don't think He did it just because I wanted the shot. If that were the case, I would be the greatest landscape photographer on the planet. I'd never have another dud trip for the rest of my life." He was smiling as he said this, as if thinking wishfully.

"So, He did or didn't do it?" I asked, matter-of-factly.

"He did it, but He did it for us."

"Us?" I questioned. "You mean you and me?"

"Us," John stated. "He did it for His children. That is what beauty is for. All this beauty exists so you and I can see His glory, His artwork. It's like an invitation to worship Him, to know Him."

"You think?" I said, softly, after a half-reflective pause.

"Absolutely, Don. Beauty doesn't make any sense apart from God giving a gift to His children. Think about it. Is there a Darwinian explanation for beauty? Not really. It's a love letter, that's all. It's this massive letter to creation inviting us to enjoy Him. I'm always telling the kids that sunsets are God's final brushstrokes on the beauty of the day."

"But why would He do that?" I asked.

"Because it is who He is. It's like with Chris," John

leaned back in his seat a bit when he thought about his son. "I do things for Chris because I know Chris will love it. We go on a hike, we go down to the river, whatever. Showing Chris things that give him pleasure also gives me pleasure. I've seen a river a thousand times; after a while, you just get bored. But when Chris and I go to the river, I live the whole thing through him. I feel his pleasure, and it gives me pleasure. So, God is like that. A father is a fitting metaphor for God."

"For some," I said cynically, rolling my eyes. John looked over and smirked, but something in his glance evidenced he suddenly remembered I didn't have a dad. I wasn't trying to make a big deal out of it. John nodded a little and hummed, though, and grabbed the steering wheel like he was thinking about something. It was a long time after that until he talked again.

Once we got up to Lost Lake, he told a story about the time he took a canoe out to try to get another angle on the mountain, then he pointed out clouds he thought might light up come sunset, but it wasn't until we hiked around to the south side of the lake and were standing on the dock that John brought up our previous conversation. And I've come back to what he said many times. He was setting up the tripod and opening the camera case, and he started talking, not really looking at me.

"You know, Don," he said, fidgeting with a lens, snapping it into the camera, and setting the whole thing atop the tripod, "sometimes I don't even think of the kids as my own kids."

I thought about that for a second. "Terri sleep with the mailman?" I joked, more or less under my breath.

"Very funny," he said, shaking his head. "I ought to throw you in the lake for that one."

"Kidding," I told him.

"I mean they are *our* kids and all," John sounded introspective as he talked, absorbed in thought while he adjusted the camera, "but really they belong to God. Terri and I had sex, but that's it. I don't know how to make a human being. God makes a human being."

"Why do you bring this up?" I asked after a minute or so of silence.

"I guess what I am saying is, one day, I've got to introduce Chris to his real Father. And I'm not talking about the mailman." I laughed as John delivered that line. "I mean God put me in Chris's life," he continued, "to take care of him and love him, but ultimately, we all belong to God. In Scripture He refers to Himself as our Father and I think He really longs for us to know Him as that. So I would say, none of us is really without a father." Again, John didn't look at me as he talked. He started focusing his camera and reading his light meter. He cupped his hands above his eyes and checked the west for color.

"Point taken," I said, mostly to break the silence.

"I don't know, Don, maybe you have to be a father to

understand it. And I think someday you will understand it. But there isn't any love like this. I love Chris and the girls in a way I can't explain. I really can't. It feels like some kind of miracle. I want them to love life; I want to give them joy; I want them to mature. And now that I have felt all this, I understand so much more of life; I understand why a sunset is beautiful; I understand why I don't get what I want all the time; I understand why God disciplines me; I understand God is a father."

At this point, some color spilled out of the west, brightening the rolling hills of evergreen, and fell across Ladd Glacier. John didn't say anything, he just pointed at the water. And in the water I could see the mountain perfectly mirrored, the point of its summit, the black crag of rock rising up like a spine on the south face. John pressed his thumb against the trigger and reached in his bag for another slide, slipping the exposed plate out of the camera, replacing it with a new plate. He waited a second, checked the upside-down image in the viewer, then snapped another picture. After this, the brilliant color faded into light purples and amethyst. John took one more shot of the less brilliant light, and then we sat on the dock and watched the sky slowly go dark.

On the drive back to the house, John was quiet. I started thinking about God as Father, wondering whether I really believed it. I had always believed God was loving and kind; and as I said before, prayer came easily to me. But, honestly,

I had a more distant picture of God than that of Father. The God in my imagination was terribly old, forgetful, not so much interacting with humanity as apathetically watching us work our jobs and mow our lawns. This idea of God fathering us was new to me, and while I confess I liked it, I didn't know if I could buy in. Maybe John was right; maybe I had to actually be a father before I could understand. But I liked the bit of hope. I liked the idea of God, up in heaven, offering guidance and counsel and reward in my life. And I liked the idea I hadn't been completely abandoned.

About the time John and I came off the forest service road, back onto the highway that snakes down Mount Hood, I remembered a commercial that used to run on television when I was a kid. It was a Lifesavers commercial that had a boy sitting on the side of a hill with his father. The father and son were watching the sunset, and as the sun descended, the father whispered to his son *going, going, going,* and as the sun finally slipped beneath the horizon, the father whispered, *gone.* Then this kid, silhouetted in the evening light, looked up at his father and said, *Do it again, Dad.*

It had been ten years since I had seen that commercial, but thinking about the things John said, and having watched purple slip down the glaciers on Mount Hood, the mountain laying its reflection against the water, I wondered about God as Father, about how He might get joy by giving us joy, the way John said he experienced this with Chris.

The idea became more appealing as we continued

driving home, because if it were true, it meant I did belong, that *all* of us belonged, that we're here on purpose. And though some of us grow up without biological fathers, none of us grows up without our actual Father. That is, if we have skin, if we have a heart that is beating and can touch and feel, then all this is because God has decided it would be so, because He wanted to include us in the story.

By the time we got back to the house, Terri and the kids were asleep. John and I sat in the den and watched Sports Center for a while. During commercials, he would mute the television and make small talk about some of the trips he had coming up, wondering out loud how he was going to get around once arriving in New Zealand, wondering how many days he should spend there as opposed to Australia. He was saying all this with some regret, and you could tell he didn't like being away from his family. But during the last commercial break, he started talking again about being a father, and I could tell he was doing it more for me than just to reminisce. He told me that when Terri gave birth to Chris, and he held his son in his arms for the first time, it was the closest he had ever been to understanding the love of God. He said that though he had never met this little person, this tiny baby, he felt incredible love for him, as though he would lie down in front of a train if he had to, that he would give up his life without so much as thinking about it, just because this child existed. John set this love beside other relationships, but they didn't compare. In other relationships, the person he knew had to earn his love. Even with his own father, John *learned* to love him; and with his wife, they had *fallen* in love over several years, becoming closer and closer friends. But it wasn't that way with his children. His love for them was instantaneous, from the moment of their birth. They had performed nothing to earn his love other than be born. It was the truest, most unconditional love he had known. John said if his love for Chris was the tiniest inkling of how God loved us then he had all the security in the world in dealing with God, because he knew, firsthand, what God's love toward him felt like, that it was complete.

"I'm just saying, Don, if God is our Father, we've got it good. We've got it really good." After that, John tossed the remote into my lap, put his glass in the sink, and said good night.

"See you in the morning," I said.

"Good night, Don," John said, the kitchen door closing behind him.

Chapter Five

SPIRITUALITY:
GOD IS FATHERING US

It feels creepy to say God is fathering us — creepy in an invasion-of-privacy sense. I mentioned before that prayer comes easily to me, but I confess I like the distant God, the God who has a firm grasp of physics but isn't so swift at relational dynamics. I see God this way most of the time, as a kind of foggy-minded scientist who never got married: too smart, really, to "get" people. You don't picture God being good with women, do you, or sitting around at a baseball game smoking a cigar, talking about the time the ball went through Buckner's legs.

I've always thought of God in conceptual terms, the way Brian Greene thinks about superstrings. Still, I find this sad. God couldn't make it clearer He wants intimacy. In Bible study once, John explained how strongly God communicates His desire for relationships. He calls Himself a bridegroom, a friend, a lover, a shepherd. An Old Testament book called Song of Songs is ripe with erotic imagery, and if you take it allegorically, it makes you wonder if God doesn't want us to be, somehow, spiritually wooed.

But God lives in heaven, not down the street. He can't play with us, as it were. I confess I often think of God like "the boy in the bubble" trying to explain to the other kids that while they can't play basketball with Him, exactly, they can still talk on the phone about comic books or something. I know I am trivializing God, and I don't mean to, but it does feel like His bigotry against our sin-germs affects His ability to bond. He doesn't hug, for example.

But the stuff John said about God fathering us stayed with me. John left for Europe for a time, shortly after our conversation, and I started wondering how, if God wanted to father us, He could do so from such intangibility. What I mean is, how does the owner and creator of the hamster cage interact with the hamsters? How could an interaction with God look anything like the interaction we're supposed to have with our earthly fathers? And worse, if our earthly fathers are God's way of communicating His love for us, then, apparently, God only loves some of us. And the way the statistics are going, fewer of us every day.

Then I began to wonder if I was pushing the "father"

metaphor too far, that perhaps the metaphor's purpose is more humble. I wondered if all the relationships we have — relationships with our lover, our mother, our friends — are not unlike blurred photos of our relationship with God, as though they are foreshadowings in the sappy prologue of an eternal novel.

I wondered if sliding our arms around a woman's hips wasn't a kind of infantile introduction to the metaphysical. If I allow myself, I can see God holding up flashcards as I fall in love with a woman, cards that say, *this is love, I am like this love, only better.*

"See," God says, pointing at the flashcard with the word "love," then pointing at His own chest while I move down the woman's lips to her chin and her neck. "See," God says, putting down the flashcard with "love" and picking up the word "oneness." He says, "Get it? Do you see? It's all living metaphors. It's a hint of oneness — like My Trinity!"

Thinking about this for too long made me dizzy. But I admit I started getting used to the idea of calling God "Father." I was ready for God to step out of anonymity. I wanted to know what John had said was true, not only as a guy who grew up without a dad, but as a human being. And as odd as all the metaphor talk may sound, thinking of human love as a metaphor for who God is helped me. It helped me know He is doing what He can for us, and it helped me realize I probably know as much about God as a baby knows the physics of the mobile dangling above his crib.

After all, the metaphors—love between a father and a son, between a man and a woman—didn't have to be exact. They were only supposed to make a motion, to *grunt* toward the inexplicable. And we don't *all* get to experience *all* the metaphors. A person who never leaves China doesn't get to appreciate God's handiwork in Yosemite National Park, but he will have his own versions there in China. This was important to me, because it meant that, even though I didn't have a dad, I still knew about love, and from plenty of places. So, while all the metaphors weren't firing, some of them were. I could still understand God was loving and kind, because I knew about love and kindness. And I could still understand Him as the Father to the fatherless, even if not firsthand.

What I am getting at is the concept of a father may have been soiled for you and me, but it was important for me to realize who did the soiling. To be fair, it wasn't God. If I take the Bible as true, then God bears none of the negative characteristics of our biological fathers. And when I think of my own father as a living flashcard rather than a mirror image, I am comforted that the One toward whom the metaphor grunts is vastly superior to the grunt itself.

So I said this out loud: I want God to father me. I'm not trying to be pious here, it's just that I knew guys who were truly fathered had certain advantages in life. They were good at sports, for example, and good with girls. They knew how to manage money better, and got their college paid for. At least some of them. So I wanted this, and even though

God lived in a bubble, I wanted Him to step out of heaven and show me how to work a power saw.

I prayed about it a little, but God never showed up. He never knocked on my door with a football under His arm, big smile from ear to ear. So I started feeling stupid for wanting Him to father me in the first place. But a few things happened that helped me understand God, how He works, who He is, and that in a way, He had been fathering me all my life. I know it all sounds like mushy new-age spirituality, like I ought to be living in a tent out in Colorado, asking a tree what I should eat for breakfast, but I'm not like that. I don't think He fathers us by putting vague notions in our minds, or talking to us through whispery winds. I am speaking in very practical terms.

John's mentioning how God worked something like a father led me on a search through the Bible. It wasn't a very deep search, because I don't know the Bible very well, but the searching I did proved worth the time. And perhaps it's just me, but it seems like no matter where I looked in the Bible, I could see God was fathering people, or doing something very much like fathering people.

The first thing I found was in the book of Romans. Paul, when he started the book, began by talking about people who decided not to have anything to do with God, and because of that, they'd all become pagans, not really knowing how to control themselves, not having any discipline. They didn't know how to be humans, really. And in a way, I knew I was kind of like those guys. I'm not evil by today's standards, and I'd not done or even thought to do many of the things Paul was talking about, but in general I felt like one of those guys because they were a bunch of people who were disassociated from their father. And when I say Father here, I am talking about God.

It sounds confusing, I know, but it made me think of those elephants again, and how they needed a bigger, older elephant to change their biochemistry and teach them how to be who they were. I wondered if this wasn't, basically, what Paul was getting at in the book of Romans. Without God being God in our lives, we are going to mess it up somehow. I guess I am also saying that we are interdependent.

It only makes sense. People who go out in the woods by themselves for a long time usually come back crazy. And it's also true that men become who they were designed to be when they interact with a woman, and vice versa for that matter. Having kids brings about another kind of maturity, too. Relationships unlock certain parts of who we are supposed to be. I think one of the things Paul might have been saying in Romans is that being in a relationship with God helps us understand who we are and become who we are designed to become. And so in a way, it seemed like God was supposed to be the bigger, older elephant to those guys who were messing everything up in Rome. And the reason they were messing up their lives is because they didn't want anything to do with Him.

———

IT HELPED ME to consider this dynamic in natural terms. About this time, I was planting a couple tomato plants in the backyard. I'd never planted anything before, but the guy across the street had planted some tomato plants the year before and that got me interested. I was digging a little hole and sticking the starter plant in the ground when the miracle of the process occurred to me. All you do is stick a plant in the dirt, and the sun and soil and a summer's worth of time turns the tomato plant into a living salad maker. Its DNA is activated by outside forces, so it becomes what it is supposed to become only in the right elements.

It's like it says in the Bible, if we know God and interact with Him, we are like a tree firmly planted by a river. And I started wondering if God's fathering us, and our paying attention to Him and obeying Him, wasn't the process we go through to produce fruit, or to become what we are supposed to become. Just like my tomato plant, for example.

But what does this look like? That's when I came across a copy of the Lord's Prayer. It was on a refrigerator magnet at a friend's house. Because I had been thinking about the fatherhood of God, the word *father* stuck out, and I stood and read through it while I was getting water. The prayer goes like this:

Our Father, Who art in heaven,
Hallowed be Thy name.
Thy kingdom come, Thy will be done
On earth as it is in heaven.
Give us this day our daily bread.
Forgive our transgressions
Even as we have forgiven our enemies.
And lead us not into temptation
But deliver us from evil.
For Thine is the kingdom and the power and the
glory forever. Amen.

I liked the fact Jesus said we could call God Father. And even though I had read that passage many times before, in this new light it felt revolutionary. Since I was a kid, I had always thought that passage was only about Jesus' attempt to teach people to pray. At my church, we would read the passage as though there were supposed to be little check boxes next to each idea you were to cover when you talked to God. For example:

1. Acknowledge God lives in heaven, and that's the One we're talking to.
2. Acknowledge His will is more important than ours.
3. Ask for daily provision, and acknowledge God is the One who provides for our needs.

4. Ask for forgiveness for our sins.

5. Forgive anybody who has been a jerk to you.

6. Ask God to keep us out of trouble.

7. Acknowledge God is great and praise Him.

The way the prayer had been explained to me, I figured if I covered all (or perhaps some) of those ideas, then my prayer would get through more clearly, and God would respond. It was like having the correct e-mail address. In other words, this was the right way to pray.

I still think something like this is true, but I wondered if there wasn't more. Reading through the passage in Matthew chapter 6 again, I looked at it the way John MacMurray had tried to teach us to read the Bible—asking who it was Jesus was talking to, what He was trying to communicate to them, and then asking if there is anything in the passage that relates to my situation. And this seemed to open the passage up a bit and answer some of my questions about how God was acting as a father.

Jesus was talking, at the time, to a mixed group of religious people. Among them were Jews, who believed a person interacted with God by obeying a system of laws. Others were Gentiles, the non-Jews. These guys, according to Jesus, were interacting with God as though He were a kind of good-luck charm. Jesus said their prayers went on and on as endless rambling. It struck me that what Jesus was doing when He gave this speech was not so much teaching people to pray as He was reminding them of what they had forgotten in the Scriptures, that we can relate to God in a personal way. I know that sounds like the same thing, but I'm wondering if I wasn't limiting Jesus' teaching by thinking it was just about behavior, and not about perspective. Jesus was saying they should stop jumping through legalistic hoops, or for that matter rambling on and on as though they could manipulate God. Instead, they should relate to God as He has always related to them, as their Father.

I read through Matthew chapter 6 several more times, and I realized Jesus was saying exactly what John had said to me out on Lost Lake, that God wants us to think of Him as a father and interact with Him as a father, and here in this passage Christ was giving us a beginner's course on how to do this. He was showing us what God does as a Divine Father, and what we should do as His children.

In so doing, Jesus radically reshaped the way I think about and interact with God.

Jesus opens His thoughts by teaching that when we pray, we should go into our inner room, and when we have shut the door, we should pray to our Father who sees in secret, and our Father who sees in secret will repay us.

That meant God was willing to be intimate with us.

In a way, Jesus was countering the trend of the time to pray loudly and in public as a way of getting other people to think we were godly. I guess back in the day women thought that was sexy or something. But praying loudly and publicly

to a vague God didn't interest Jesus at all. His use of the word
Father is unreserved and strong. This marks a sharp contrast
to the religious norm that Jesus encountered, which had
reduced God to an impersonal deity of rules and rituals.

And what's more, Jesus was telling us this relationship with the Father was supposed to be sincere and intimate. The people hearing Jesus must have been somewhat
surprised. Their Father was not afraid to be close.

The first thing God seemed to want, in terms of our
relating to Him as a father, was for us to submit to Him. *Thy
kingdom come, Thy will be done, on earth as it is in heaven,*
Jesus says. And I don't think Jesus was saying God was a
control freak, trying to make Himself feel powerful. He
could do that by smashing atoms together if He wanted;
rather, in asking us to submit, it seemed to me Jesus was
saying, *Look, you are going to want to do things your way,
but your way isn't the best for you. Trust me, I know what you
need.* Jesus had set this idea up in the previous paragraph,
saying our Father in heaven knows what we need before we
even ask Him.

I know submitting to authority isn't the most popu-
lar thing to do these days, but the thing about fathers, at
least in John MacMurray's case, is they always have their
kids' interest at heart. That concept alone changed everything for me. If God was fathering me, and He knew exactly
what I needed, then when I didn't get something I wanted,
I could trust God didn't give it to me because it was not

something I needed. I think that is part of what Jesus meant when He said, *Thy will be done.*

Here is how this idea played out in the MacMurray house. Every evening around six, Terri would set dinner on the table, and the family would sit down to eat. And every night, almost without fail, the kids would start to whine. Unless it was chicken nuggets and French fries, there were going to be problems at dinner. One evening, Cassy, who was quite good at lobbying the family for what she wanted, lay down on the kitchen floor and rolled over in frustration about having to eat whatever it was Terri had prepared. John stood at the corner of the island in the kitchen and watched her, trying not to laugh. She twisted and turned and moaned and complained, but John stood silently, not letting her manipulate him. Finally, Cassy belted out the now famous line: "Dad, how could you do this to me?" John and I covered our mouths and looked away in hysterics.

But here is what is so interesting about that scene. Cassy actually believed what she was saying had merit. The pain and frustration she felt about dinner that night was the same pain and frustration you and I probably feel about not getting the job we want, the car we want, or whatever. Looking back, it struck me how often I have wondered, sometimes out loud to God, *How could you do this to me?*

In the situation with Cassy, John had some choices as a father. One thing he could have done was to throw the dinner out and cook up some chicken nuggets and fries. But let's be honest, kids whose parents do this for them end up as evil dictators in small countries. Giving Cassy what she wanted rather than what she needed should not be confused with good parenting. If God was withholding something I wanted, it meant I could trust Him rather than cry out, *How could you do this to me?*

Instead, what John did with Cassy was to explain she could roll around on the kitchen floor all day but she still wasn't going to get her way. She was, in fact, going to stand up, go to the table, and eat with the rest of the family, even if it took all night. He was going to father her toward maturity.

Nobody would watch John interact with Cassy that way and say He was an unloving father. There was no diminished affection between Cassy and John. In fact, his giving Cassy what she needed rather than what she wanted was, in itself, an act of love.

In the Lord's Prayer, after Jesus tells us we need to submit to God, He says that God is going to provide, that we can trust Him to provide what we need, even down to the basics of food. To me, that seems to build on what Jesus had just said about trusting God to give us what we need for maturity rather than what we want.

Give us this day our daily bread, Jesus said.

I could be wrong, but I think Jesus is talking about much more than food. I think He is talking about keeping us alive, sustaining us. I think that passage is an acknowledgment of God's ability to provide security. In the years I lived with the MacMurrays, I never encountered Chris out in the woods with his BB gun hunting for dinner. Dinner was always on the table around six, and John and Terri were more than happy to provide.

I was e-mailing with an old friend recently, whom I hadn't heard from in about ten years. In the time since we talked, my friend Dean had gotten married and had two children. We exchanged pleasantries for a few e-mails, talking about where we were working and what we had been doing since we last talked, and then I asked him about his family. And in a tender e-mail, Dean explained how much his children had changed his view of himself and his life. He talked about how, on days he did not feel like getting out of bed and going to work, he would hear one of his sons' voices in the hall or the giggling from their room, and it was enough to get him into the shower and into his suit. He loved his kids and was motivated to provide for their happiness and health. Their having good food to eat and books to read and movies to see mattered more than his comfort. Dean explained that he wouldn't want it any other way, that what was once mundane (having to work) became beautiful because the motives had changed. And I wondered as I read Dean's e-mail how much of God we see in the heart of a good father, loving and providing for his children.

As I stopped to think about it, even the idea of God providing each day could be seen as an invitation to intimacy. He wants us to depend on Him, to lean on Him, to realize our smallness in the reality of His bigness. Our provision comes from God, Jesus seems to be saying, and in our asking we are realizing the love He displays in His willingness to provide. It was a sobering idea to realize, which I suppose is the reason Jesus wants the concept to come up in our prayers. I felt grateful after thinking about how God provides. It sounds silly to say it, but it made me like God more.

Jesus then goes on to explain we are to forgive our debtors even as we have been forgiven.

John MacMurray would say the idea God has forgiven us is in many ways the crux of Christian spirituality. God has forgiven our sins, and we shouldn't be holding out on other people when we have been forgiven something so huge. But looking at this passage through the lens of a child wondering what his father wants, it seems like Jesus is striking a familiar MacMurray family theme. Unity is huge with John and Terri. They are always telling the kids not to fight. Chris isn't allowed to put Elle's head in the fan, for instance. I don't know how many times I saw John kneel down and put his arms around one of his daughters, whispering in her ear, guiding her through the process of asking and giving forgiveness to one of her siblings. The kids had to learn how to live together. It doesn't come naturally. If they weren't guided in this process, and if it wasn't a family rule, they would become isolated and defensive, and they wouldn't grow into maturity. And so it seemed beautiful that God would want us to get along, to forgive each other and accept forgiveness. And it also seemed beautiful that God wasn't just my Father, concerned with my maturity, but He was *our* Father, concerned with the unity and health of the whole family.

Perhaps I am reading too much into the Lord's Prayer. But I don't think so. If anything, I think I had been reading too little into it all those years. I think the passage clearly demonstrates a Father-child relationship. And, like I was saying, these ideas made me grateful.

The prayer ends with some important praise—an admission, if you will, of who does what in the relationship we have with God. Jesus says, "For *Thine* is the kingdom and the power and the glory, forever and ever. Amen."

I suppose if I were trying to teach this idea to children, I might simply ask them to pray, "God, you are great big. You are bigger than everything, and that is amazing. You are the one with the power, and You always will be."

———

HERE IS HOW this broke down after having thought about it for a long time: I used to feel a kind of hopelessness about life. I assumed life was against me, that whatever bad could happen to a person was going to happen to me. It was as though there was a current I was swimming against. But it was studying this passage that changed some of that thinking. God is fathering me. God is fathering us. I know that if God loves me and wants me to succeed as much as John loves his kids and wants them to succeed, then life cannot be hopeless.

But another idea that occurred to me was I needed to change the way I understand spirituality. What I mean is, I needed to allow God to father me. I needed to acknowledge him as Father and submit. Traditional language might use the term repentance here. In part, this meant admitting I wanted autonomy from God, admitting I wanted my own way, and asking Him to change my heart. One of the issues I deal with having grown up without a father is a kind of resentment at the mention of actually needing a dad. I had to admit I needed one. I had to tell God I wanted Him to father me.

One of the most tender and beautiful scenes that would occasionally unfold in the MacMurray house was the calm, quiet peace that would come over one of the children when they were done trying to get their way. Cassy would get up off the floor and walk over to where her dad was and hold out her arms, her face still pouting. Then, John would sit down on the couch and hold her and rock her in his arms. If John had scolded Chris about something and sent him to his room, Chris would come out later and walk over to John while he was sitting on the couch and climb into his arms, burying his head in his neck. Sometimes it was as if the kids were saying they were sorry, not yet old enough to know how to express themselves with words. But at other times, and perhaps more tender times, the kids were still frustrated, still confused about why they couldn't get what they wanted or why they seemed to always be getting into trouble; and the embrace, the coming to John and burying themselves in his arms was more about feeling his love *in* the confusion, *in* the difficulty, than it was about having moved past it. It was as if they were asking him if he still loved them, if the discipline meant there was anything lost in their much-needed relationship with their father. There wasn't. Discipline is what a Father does, *because* He loves.

————

HERE'S SOMETHING ELSE I noticed John do with his kids. Chris and Elle were arguing one time, and John felt like he raised his voice too loud in telling them to knock it off. Not long after that, maybe a few minutes, he went to them and told them he was sorry for yelling. They didn't seem to care, and it wasn't a big deal, but for some reason it stuck in my mind as an interesting thing for a father to do. I asked him about it the last time we talked, and John said he tries to apologize when he messes up as a dad, letting his kids know they are more important to him than his pride. He kind of laughed and admitted he screwed up fairly often. But then he said something I thought was pertinent to those of us who grew up without dads. John said another reason he apologized was because he didn't want his kids to have any negative perceptions about God. He said that the way a kid feels about their dad is sometimes projected onto God, so if he apologized when he messed up as a father, the kids would know that was his mistake, and didn't have anything to do with who God is. Or at least that is what he hoped.

I liked that idea, because it reaffirmed that our fathers aren't God. They can help us understand who God is and how good He is, but they can also do a lot of damage. But God is God regardless, and if we take the Bible as true, it's good to think He is fathering us perfectly.

There is this great text in the Bible that says, essentially, if our earthly fathers know how to love us, just imagine how great God's love is. I take this to mean that even a very good earthly father is no comparison to God.

There is a part of me, and I think it is a growing part, that believes if I submit to God, read the Bible and obey His commands, and also talk to Him about stuff going on in my life, in His own way, He is fathering me toward maturity.

And there is something profoundly humbling about knowing God. I'm not talking about the trinket God or the genie-in-a-lamp God, I mean the God who invented the tree in my front yard, the beauty of my sweetheart, the taste of a blueberry, the violence of a river at flood. I think there are a lot of religious trends that would have us controlling God, telling us that if we do this and that and another, God will jump through our hoops like a monkey. But this other God, this real God, is awesome and strong, all-encompassing and passionate, and for reasons I will never understand, He wants to father us.

Chapter Six

AUTHORITY:
THE THING ABOUT CHOPPY AIR

When I was younger, I didn't trust older men. And it's only in the last few years I've understood why. I know I was more or less an awkward kid growing up, a few years behind in maturity, always having some kind of show-off show going on, and I don't think a lot of the men I knew back then had a great deal of tolerance for me. My grandfather died when I was a kid, and my dad, of course, had taken off before I was old enough to walk. Then one of my uncles left my aunt, and my other uncle had kids of his own to raise on the other side of the country, so the immediate family had no men at all. No men and no boys, just me and a lot of women.

Being a guy, of course, I felt out of place, but I didn't feel any more comfortable standing around with a group of men, either. When hanging out with my friends and their dads, I knew I didn't belong. There is something about having your own father standing there talking to your friends' fathers that validates you: You're *his* kid, not just some stray that wandered in off the street. So, although I never knew it at the time, I grew up with a constant feeling of insecurity, even a fear there was a consequence for being who I was, a kind of subconscious knowing that I wasn't okay, and someday I was going to pay for it. This feeling I didn't fit in gave me a noticeable distrust of authority, especially of older men.

Sometimes I think the reason we don't like certain people is because we feel insecure around them. We like to chalk it up to political or philosophical differences, maybe, but the truth is, if we are honest, we are drawn to those who validate us and affirm us, and we resist those who don't.

Because I didn't have a father, I felt there was a club of men I didn't belong to. I would have never admitted it at the time, but I wanted to belong. I desperately wanted to belong. At the father-and-son campout, I knew Matt wasn't my dad, and I knew he probably didn't want to be there. I knew he was slightly embarrassed that in a group of men who were bonding with their sons, he was walking around with a charity case. I couldn't have put words to it back then, but I felt it. Every time I met an older man, I assumed he would not like me, and he would not want me around.

I felt as though all the men in the world secretly met in some warehouse late at night to talk about man things, to have secret handshakes, to discuss how great it was to have a penis and what an easy thing it was to operate, how to throw a football or a baseball, how to catch a fish and know what kind it was, and be able to grab it and stop its flapping around, doing this without jolting their heads back or squinting their eyes. They talked about how to look a woman in the eye and tell her she was your woman and that she looks good in that dress and make it so your eyes say you love her but you could survive without her, and how to drive a stickshift truck without grinding the gears. And then I secretly believed at the end of the meeting they gathered around and reminded each other that under no circumstances was anybody to tell *me* about these things.

Absurd, I know. I say this because when you grow up believing an entire community of men have a fraternity you are not allowed into, you don't like them, or their club, and you tend to defend your manhood by awkwardly trying to knock up cheerleaders. Or you try to become a man by getting into fights in bars. Or you just give up completely, and you silently harbor bitterness toward the idea of manhood all together. And you hate men who look anything like authority. You hate them because they first hated you.

Sometimes I think if a person has parents who speak love into their life, they end up with a personality that trusts others more easily, feels more comfortable, gives and takes with authority and so on. There is a good chance you and I didn't learn that trust. I've thought a lot about why I struggled so much with authority, and the best reason I've come up with is that the insecurities I felt were compounded by the tone of impersonal indifference I sensed coming from positions of power. The natural reaction to indifference is resistance, cynicism, bitterness, hurt, and so on, and without a father figure representing positive authority, all authority became suspect, and communication with the God-given guides became strained.

I didn't show this mistrust on the surface. I could get along pretty well, but the bitterness was there, deep, and it affected things quite negatively. If I were working for a man, for example, and he came out and barked some orders at me and then went back into his office, I would spend the rest of the day imagining myself walking off the job. I would assume, at the beginning of the relationship, the guy thought I was a loser and couldn't measure up. A normal kid with a healthy identity would probably jump to the task and earn the guy's respect, really show him he is a man, because he *knows* he is a man. In those instances, however, I would end up loafing around trying to get away with being paid without working. I am not proud of it now, but I didn't know any better. What I mean is, this is who I thought I was.

As I grew older, the condition got worse. I organized my life so I didn't have to submit to anybody, and even found myself getting angry with any man who wanted to impose rules. And when you grow up in a church, there are a million men who want to impose rules. Throw a rock and you will hit a guy looking down his nose at some other guy who isn't "acting right." And I think I assumed anybody twenty years older who wanted to tell me what to do just wanted to use me so he could feel powerful.

In my life, there has never been a connection between authority and love. Even with John MacMurray, who was certainly an authority figure, there wasn't the kind of love I needed. A father is a father is a father, and there isn't any substitute. I would get mad at John, bitter sometimes, and I never knew why. He would ask me to do something, to take out the trash or whatever, and as soon as he left the room the anger would surface in my chest, feelings of bitterness and resentment, and I wanted nothing more than to dump the can of trash on the front lawn.

That was really the beginning of some hard and dark thinking for me. I didn't want to admit I had a problem with authority. And even in the times when I could admit it, those same difficult feelings were there, that the very people who were handing down advice didn't like me, didn't have a stake in whether or not my life was going to turn out well, and there was certainly no love, not deep love, not unconditional love.

Everything intensified during the years I lived with John and his family. I haven't told you everything. There were times I hated John. And it's not like he had a bunch of rules or anything. John barely had any rules. But, like I was saying, I operated out of this sense of rejection, unable to understand that John was not my father and wasn't supposed to love me like a father.

Of the four years I lived with John and Terri, this is my single regret. I wish I had known I could have trusted John. That is, I wish I could have respected John and appreciated him *in his place*, as a friend, a mentor, and nothing more. If I could have done this, I would have clearly seen how much he was for me.

If you think about it, this distrust of authority creates a fierce succession of difficulties. If I put myself in John's shoes, he has no choice but to think I am a bad kid. I mean, he is doing everything he can — mentoring me, letting me live at his place, including me in a small way in his family — and yet I was, in many ways, ungrateful. I would magnify any quirk in John's personality, practically demonizing him.

Here is the real truth I am stammering toward. John MacMurray isn't my father. My boss isn't my father. The cop on the street isn't my father. My father split, and that stinks, and none of these guys are going to replace him. And what that means is that they are not responsible to love me unconditionally, and they aren't responsible to tell me I am a man. Any love or affirmation they give is a gift, but holding them responsible for the insult my father cast down is inappropriate. The wound I have isn't there because of them.

———

I WAS ON a plane a few years ago, flying from Chicago to Portland, and I happened to plug my headphones into the jack on the armrest. On a plane, you can sometimes listen to the radio transmissions coming in and out of the cockpit. I was curious about what pilots say to each other, so like a good geek, I listened for a while. It turns out most of the transmissions are about weather and whether or not the plane is heading for choppy air. The pilot would radio to a plane that was en route an hour or so ahead of us and get a report on what kind of turbulence they were experiencing; then, he would turn and radio the plane that had just taken off in Chicago to explain what sort of air we were flying through at the moment. The system was primitive, but intelligent. Planes fly from Chicago to Portland all day, and all day they are handing back warnings and forecasts, keeping everybody safe and comfortable.

It occurred to me, listening to the pilots talk to each other, how much this was like life. I know it sounds simple, but at the time, it came as a revelation. I could see it clearly, the fact that in life there are people being born, just as others are passing away. And all the way through, the guys who are twenty years ahead are teaching the guys twenty years behind what kind of weather they will be encountering at whatever stage of life they happen to be living in. And I couldn't help but wonder if, perhaps, my distrust of authority was costing me something.

I started thinking about the wisdom that is handed down when we have authority figures in our lives. We learn a trade by submitting to authority, we learn a work ethic by submitting to authority, we gain an academic life by submitting to authority, and more than any of this, we learn who we actually are by submitting to authority. And when we have earned authority ourselves, we teach others, because for so many years we have been taught. A guy like me, then, who has a resistance to authority, is begging to be useless. What I mean is, he isn't receiving any advice on how to live, and in turn he isn't able to hand advice down to those who are coming behind him. And if he *is* handing down advice, it isn't good advice. I mean it isn't tested and tried by years of experience.

When I made the connection between the pilots taking off and landing, passing back information, and the span of a life, an older man passing back wisdom to a younger man, I wondered who I was receiving wisdom from. And I couldn't think of one person. Not one. I immediately assumed this was because men in authority didn't like me. But I was getting too old to still believe that.

It took a long time to connect the fact I didn't like authority with the idea I felt older men were rejecting me, and even longer to realize I was really looking for the kind of validation I should have received from a father, the kind of validation no man is going to give except to his own son. And that's a bum deal for guys like you and me.

I realized, however, there is not a secret meeting of men who weren't teaching me the confidential handshake. Men are just men, and half of them are scared and wondering if they are doing life right anyway. I had to ask for a great deal of forgiveness. Once I understood authority had its place, I started realizing how much I could benefit by seeking advice from those who were in front of me.

I still have some problems with authority, but it's funny how much of the anger has gone away. I've learned to avoid authority figures who aren't submitting to anybody themselves. What good is the wisdom of a man who has nobody speaking into his life? And I've found if you sit down with a man you trust and respect and explain to him you never learned about some area of life, girls or money, cars or computers, you would be amazed at how honored they are to help. They practically pour out their lives, for heaven's sake. I sit down every once in a while with men who are twenty and thirty years older than me, and I ask them if they see any blind spots in my life, character flaws and that sort of thing. The answers that come back are always encouraging, and I can hear in the voices of these men, and see in their eyes, they want me to succeed, they want me to make it and to thrive.

I know my father took off a long time ago, but there isn't any reason this should ruin my life more than it has to. It wasn't easy, but I'm hearing the warnings now, and I'm learning to stay clear of choppy air.

Chapter Seven

MANHOOD:
THE RIGHT EQUIPMENT

Many years ago, I attended something called a Promise Keepers rally. This was an event where thousands of men gathered in a football stadium to shout cheers about how much they loved God. There was more to it than that, of course, but this was the most noticeable characteristic. It was strictly a religious thing, but I liked it. All the men at the Promise Keepers rally were supposed to sign a contract, swearing under God, they would interact with other races, pray all the time, and refrain from yelling at their wives and kids. I went to the rally the second year they were held, back when Promise Keepers was becoming a movement, and even though I didn't have a wife or kid to yell at, I found the event moving. It made me feel like I was working on my manhood, becoming a better person, sitting and listening to lectures and taking notes and scribbling down ideas—actionable steps I could follow that would make my spiritual manhood more pronounced. Each lecture included lists we were supposed to make and accountability to get the stuff on our lists done. I didn't know becoming a man involved so much paperwork, to be honest.

The concept of manhood was relatively new to me. Perhaps because I grew up without the consistent influence of any man, I wasn't aware there was a unique identity that only men could feel. I knew we were stronger, in general, and our lies come more to the surface, but other than this, I didn't know the distinctions. And when I learned about the distinctions, I rather liked them. I felt, in a way, the Promise Keepers rally helped me understand experientially what a man is supposed to do, what a man is supposed to feel like. And I absorbed the rituals, and I cheered with the cheering, and I noted my notes, and all the while felt as though it was a kind of rite of passage. I was a man, I supposed, because I had attended the rally. I had paid my money and the person at the ticket booth did not hesitate in handing me a pass.

But the feeling of manhood was short-lived. As part of our agreement with God, we were supposed to be actively involved in a Bible study, which I did not do. There was a Bible study at my church, but there were women in it, which compromised the "manhood" purpose, so I stopped attending. And we were supposed to include black people in our lives, and I was excited about this until I realized I didn't know any black people. When I approached them at the mall and explained my dilemma, they looked at me confused.

In the long run, the experiment was a flop. I do hold out hope, however, that I will never yell at my wife or kids. At present this is easy because I do not have a wife or kids. As a rule, I do not yell at the wives or children of my friends, and I feel this is good practice for a wife and kids of my own, but they say there is nothing like the real thing to test a man's character. Regardless, the Promise Keepers rally left me in a quandary: I was awakened to the idea there was such a thing as a real man, a God's man, a man's man, but since I hadn't kept any of the promises, a growing doubt was seeded that I might not be the real thing. If there is one thing the Promise Keepers rally insinuated, it was that there were real men and fake men. They even sold bumper stickers that stated "Real Men Love Jesus," and as hopeful as I was that I fit this definition, I secretly knew I wasn't that kind of Christian. I wasn't the kind of Christian who was good at keeping rules.

And if I were honest with myself, I would have admitted I didn't know exactly what a man was. The rally taught me what a man does, and how loud a man must cheer, but apart from shallow bumper-sticker logic, Promise Keepers didn't define the term. I found myself looking for a general definition. Because, if I had a general definition of a man, I would know whether or not I was one.

I attended a church in the suburbs after this and finally found a men's gathering where they talked about hunting and eating wild game, and I would sit there feeling like an idiot, pretending to be amused by stories about shooting deer, and how somebody's buddy rushed into a cave and killed a bear while it was sleeping. The truth is I was never amused. I wasn't even interested. And even though my best friend Roy and I went fishing a great deal when I was a kid, I was never that much into it. For me fishing was just something to do with a friend. I never went hunting, either, and I was not groomed for sports. I liked war movies some, but I liked human drama movies more, movies like *The Breakfast Club* or *The Karate Kid*—movies where geeks prevailed against great social odds so they could date cheerleaders. But when all the football analogies started up at the men's group, and all the talk was about how, in our spiritual lives, we are like characters in the latest bloodfest movie, except we only get to kill people metaphorically, I just wasn't feeling it. So, I continued wondering if I was one of the guys, wondering if I was really a man. I wondered why they couldn't speak to somebody on my level. I thought, for example: Why not have a men's meeting where we talked about how Duckie got to kiss Molly Ringwald in *Pretty in Pink*, and how someday we were all going to kiss Molly Ringwald, metaphorically?

I knew if we were to break into small groups and the guys were to start telling stories about how faith is like killing a sleeping bear, my contribution about how faith is like the last Cure record wasn't going to motivate anybody.

And so for a long time I wandered around in a fog. Manhood felt like something that had been handed to me accidentally. I just knew somebody was going to explain I was actually a lesbian with a penis, and if I wanted I could continue to watch college football, but should probably tone down the interest in post-season baseball, as this territory was reserved for men who had killed sleeping bears. Or for men who loved Jesus.

But feelings of rejection always turn into feelings of resentment, and shortly I began begrudging the fact I was made to feel unmanly. I started thinking about how stupid you would have to be to believe life is like an *Alien* sequel and Jesus was like a boxer with a Philadelphia accent. I couldn't sit through men's meetings anymore without rolling my eyes, or, at the end of prayers, sarcastically replacing the common phrase *Amen* with a loud and guttural *Git 'er Dun*. I mockingly wore NASCAR shirts to the meetings and made up stories about how I had spent the last two days stalking rabid squirrel on the Pacific Crest Trail. *Them's tasty critters*, I'd say in my best hick accent. *Common squirrels keep fat off so they can balance on telephone lines, but mountain squirrels can get big as housecats. . . .*

To my surprise, my commodity rose at Bible study and I was soon asked to teach. I did a series called *The Cheerleaders Are in the Wrong End Zone!* about how sluts in the Bible brought down godly men. You can't fake shallow manhood for long, though, and pretty soon the pastor discovered I had the whole John Hughes collection on DVD and suspended me from teaching indefinitely.

Once again, I felt excluded.

I began to wonder, though, if there wasn't some kind of male spirit God put in a man that was more general—something that would include men who had killed sleeping bears, for sure, but also the rest of us. I knew none of this was scientific, but here's what I meant: Women have a kind of general spirit, very sweet and kind, beautiful like a flower. In a guy there is something else, more like the spirit of a tractor or a calculator. And moreover, I wondered how that spirit was confirmed, how a person knew he had it.

———

I TOLD YOU already that my best friend when I was a kid was named Roy. Roy's father was a man's man, a fisherman who worked the oil rigs in the gulf of Mexico. He had an enormous, orange, tool container out in the backyard, a steel contraption so heavy you needed a forklift to move it. Roy and his father would stay in the backyard till all hours, working on their boat or fixing their car. The inside of Roy's house belonged to his mother, so it always smelled like roses or peanut-butter cookies, but the backyard belonged to the men, and it smelled like oil and dead fish. I used to go over and sit on a tire to talk to Roy while he lay under his dad's car, handing his father tools. And even though Roy was a couple years younger than me, he seemed to have a kind of knowing, a knowing that if he were asked to do something only a man could do, he could do it. It was a knowing I didn't have, the knowing I discovered I didn't have at the Promise Keepers rally. I know now that the reason Roy had the knowing and I didn't have the knowing was because he had a father to confirm his manhood. I found from experience you can't pick up the knowing at a Promise Keepers rally, or at a wild-game dinner. You need something more.

The idea that manhood is passed down from father to son has been an unpleasant thought. A writer named John Eldredge talks about this in his book *Wild at Heart*. He says we all carry a "father wound," and unless our father convinces us we have what it takes, we are probably going to flounder for a while. The first time I read *Wild at Heart* I threw it across the room. I hated that book, and hated anybody who told me I was less of anything because I grew up without a father. My roommate at the time loved the book, though, and on a long walk home from a coffee shop one night, he kindly explained the book goes on to talk about how God wants to heal the father wound, and how our identity as men comes from Him, how He steps in when our fathers step out. I picked it up again and read through it intensely. I won't go into the book for you here, but it's a good read and I highly recommend it. What I want to talk about, though, is how I got the knowing without getting it from my father.

The thing I believe about manhood now is that it lives within the male from a very early age, and sometimes it gets awakened, and sometimes it doesn't. It doesn't matter how old you are — a man is a man is a man.

I used to think manhood began in your late fifties, that until then it was okay to sit around and play video games, but I saw something a few years ago that changed my mind. My mom used to go into the ghettos south of Houston to bring bubble gum to underprivileged children. She would get a bucket of bubble gum and on Saturday, in all that unbelievable heat, would go door to door to trailers where migrant farm-worker families set up makeshift homes; boards leaning against barns, broken-down vans with mattresses where the seats were supposed to go, trailers half ripped apart by hurricanes, the smell of poverty. Mom would go looking for kids, handing them a piece of bubble gum, then she would tell their parents, in whatever Spanish she could muster up, that she wanted to come back the next morning and take the kids to church. She was going to come by in a bus, my mom would say, and they should be standing near the road. The next day mom would take an old school bus and pick up a load of kids, sometimes more than seventy on one bus, then take them back to the church and teach them about the Bible.

One Saturday I went with her to visit a family whose trailer had been destroyed by fire. The family was in the process of moving into another trailer, a tiny thing that was to house more than ten people. My mother heard the family needed a washing machine, and was working to have one delivered. We walked up to the house and were greeted by a child perhaps ten years old. Within seconds, though, I could tell this was no ordinary child. I felt in his handshake and in the confidence in his voice he was an equal. He stood at the top of the steps and told his little sisters, who were playing in the yard, to stay out of the mud. He talked to them with the authority and kindness of a father. The boy's mother came to the door and he translated for her in Spanish, explaining this was the woman who was going to bring the washing machine. The boy told his mother he would take care of the delivery and she shouldn't worry about it, then turned to thank my mother and me, explaining this was something they needed and it would help the family immensely. I completely forgot we were dealing with a child.

I immediately began to wonder about my own immaturity at this age. When I was this child's age I spent my time fishing in the creek by the railroad tracks or playing video games. In my teenage years, my greatest concerns were whether or not I fit in at school or if my car was cool. I rode an emotional roller coaster, wondering if I was going to fail a test I hadn't studied for.

And it was remembering this kid that caused me to disagree with the whole "Real Men Love Jesus" shtick. The kid may have loved Jesus, I have no idea, but it was at that moment I realized a lot of people are misled by believing they aren't a man unless they read some book or walk through some steps or subscribe to some religion. Don't get me wrong: I happen to be somebody who has realized I need Jesus, and I have even come to love Jesus, but I don't think somebody who doesn't love Jesus is any less of a man than somebody who does. I don't think being a "real man" has anything to do with loving Jesus at all, anymore than being a ferret has something to do with riding a bicycle.

I spent a lot of time believing I wasn't a man because I didn't like football analogies, or because I didn't want to put a cheesy bumper sticker on my car, or, well, because I didn't have a father. In a way, the guys who are promoting this approach to manhood are pretty innocent. I realize they are just trying to keep guys from yelling at their wives. But when those tactics hit my insecurities, they created a twinge. Tell a guy who grew up without a father that he is not a man unless . . . and he will automatically assume he isn't one. I didn't need manipulation. I needed affirmation.

The conclusion I have come to is more logical than emotional. It isn't my fault my dad split, and it isn't my fault my identity as a man had never been affirmed. I had to believe in the face of doubt. I had to accept the terms "man," "manliness," and "manhood" as biological terms, and while the sales tactics played on emotions, what I had to focus on was facts. Here's what I mean:

I was asked to speak to a group of 900 guys a couple years ago. They were in high school, mostly, so I started the session by asking the group what a real man was.

"How would you define a real man?" I asked the group, all of them sitting quietly. A hand slowly went up.

"A real man is somebody who provides for his family," the kid said, rather sheepishly.

"Okay, that is good," I confirmed. "That is something a 'good' man does, but I don't think you have to do that to be a (real) man. Anybody else?"

"A real man is honest, he doesn't lie," a kid shouted out.

"Very good. But again, I would say this is something a good man does, but not a qualifier for what makes a man a man. Who else wants to play?"

"A real man drives a truck!" a kid shouted out sarcastically. The group laughed.

"Not the qualifier I am looking for," I laughed back.

The group got quiet for a while as it was obvious they weren't coming up with the right answer.

"Okay," I said, "Take out a sheet of paper, because I am going to give you the definition of a real man. And you are going to want to come back to this over the next several years, because there are going to be times when you will wonder whether you are a real man, and here is a sure way to find out." After I said this I waited for everybody to get out their pens.

"Let me give you God's definition of a real man. I have searched through the Bible, and I have thought a great deal

about it, and I think I have come up with the perfect qualifier. If you have this thing, then, according to God, you are a
real man." The group looked at me anxiously, some of them
knowing, intrinsically, that whatever I said, they would be
up for the job, and some of them, quite honestly, looking at
me knowing whatever I said would exclude them.

"God's definition of a real man . . ." I said, motioning
for them to write it down

". . . is . . ." I continued.

". . . a person . . .," and I paused dramatically, waiting
for everybody to catch up.

". . . with . . .," I said, pausing again, preparing the room
for the last line, the ultimate qualifier of a man, the sure sign
that God in heaven had spoken, that God in His infinite
wisdom and perfection had endorsed them as men.

". . . a person with . . .," I repeated, waiting again until
every eye was looking at me, and then I let the cat out of
the bag.

". . . a penis!"

And as I said this, jaws dropped. Some of the kids in
the back immediately started snickering, kids on the front
row looked at me confused, some of the adults in the room
dropped their pencils. And then, slowly, the snickers in the
back of the room turned to laughter, and the laughter made
its way to the front.

And as much fun as I was having, I was also being serious. It had been a long journey for me, a journey filled with

doubt and fear, and the only answer I could come up with is that all the commercials, all the sales tactics that said I wasn't a real man unless I bought some book, or wore some after-shave, or slept with some cheerleader, were complete lies. If you have a penis, I told the group of guys, God has spoken.

I told the story of the kid from the ghetto back in Houston who was leading his family, and how whatever it is God puts in a man has been in all of us since we were young, and how the wealth of our country has caused something called "suspended adolescence," so that some of us haven't stepped into the truth that we are men—instead we are still living like children. But, what I really wanted everybody in the room to know was that they were men. So I told them. I asked them to look me in the eye, and I told them, *You are men. Some of you have never heard this before, but I want to tell you, you are men. You are not boys, you are not children, you are not women, you are men. God has spoken, and when God speaks, the majority has spoken. You are a man.*

I normally don't get so preachy, but I knew how pain-ful the journey could be, and how some guys will never really believe. I found out later that more than half the guys at the event were not living in a home with their biological fathers. There's no telling what kind of messages they were getting about who they really were.

The hard truth is, though, just because God made us men doesn't mean we are done. I know the journey of a man is difficult, and that there are forces that are always against us. I enjoy reading books about manhood, as long as they don't use manipulative sales talk. There are a number of books on this subject by guys who are actively trying to help us understand this journey. There will be times reading these books when we are tempted to believe we don't have what it takes, but I doubt very seriously any author is trying to create an exclusive club that cuts us out of membership. Elaborating on how to navigate the journey of manhood is not something I know more about than these guys, but I think it bears repeating that, if God has spoken, the journey belongs to you and me as much as it belongs to a man who grew up with a father. And it's a journey we are on whether we like it or not.

For me, the idea God has spoken is an enormous relief. If I begin to doubt my manhood, if I doubt I have what it takes, I simply have to duck into the nearest bathroom and check my shorts. If God has spoken, then I have within me whatever it takes to do the things a man needs to do, to become a good man for a woman, for some kids, for an office, for whatever it is God wants me to do.

Chapter Eight

MAKING DECISIONS:
HOW TO STAY OUT OF PRISON

My friend Travis told me a year ago he has a fear he will some day go to prison. Till then, I had never met anybody besides me with this same fear. Travis doesn't get into trouble, and I don't get into much trouble either, but both of us have a fright one day we are going to get locked up. With me, it's mostly been about traffic tickets and not paying taxes.

I didn't pay taxes for a few years. I started making some money and finally sat down with an accountant to help fill out the forms; but even with her help it was pure hell. I can't stand forms. And I used to be terrible about paying traffic tickets, not because there are forms involved but because this involves writing a check, which is a kind of form. I've had my car towed more times than I can count. I used to get tickets in the mail, notices and things, and I remember thinking if I didn't actually open the envelope then the ticket wouldn't apply to me. That's not exactly what I thought, but I sort of *felt* this was true. The letters would find piles on my dresser or next to my bed and I wouldn't pay attention to them.

Most people like me get married and their wives help them with that stuff, but I am not married and none of the women I know want to go through my mail. I never went to jail for any of this, but I always thought I might, and I still have a fear my past will come knocking on the door wearing a uniform and holding an outstanding warrant from Kansas or that weekend in Georgia.

I am still somewhat irresponsible, but it isn't as bad as it used to be. I forget to pay a credit card bill every once in a while, but I do all the big stuff. You can automate most of this these days, but that is hardly the point. I learned to make good decisions.

What I am saying is there had to come a point when I started taking responsibility for my life. I had to start open-ing envelopes, even if I didn't feel like it. I had to, because if I didn't I knew I would become one of these guys whose car is filled with newspapers and fast-food wrappers and stuffed animals in the back window. It's not just opening mail that I had to deal with. I had to show up for work on time. I had to pay taxes. I had to get car insurance. It's hard to believe I spent ten years of my life in an irresponsible fog, just kind of feeling that if I ignored the demands they would go away, or I could plead ignorance. But the hard truth is the demands don't change, they just get bigger, more adult, and the consequences of neglect get worse until pretty soon everything comes crashing down. For me, it happened at the Internal Revenue Service office downtown, sitting across the desk from a slightly sexy pencil-pusher who wasn't the least bit impressed with my monologue about having to navigate a linear universe from the cockpit of my right brain:

"I've never been much of a math person, you see. I prefer poetry. Do you read poetry? I like Dylan Thomas quite a bit, but you look like a romantic to me, Byron and all that jazz."

The lady leaned back in her chair, crossed her legs and spoke monotone, without emotion. "You owe us seventeen thousand, three hundred dollars, and ninety-three cents," she said, tilting her head slowly to the side as if she had delivered a line of verse.

"Shakespeare?" I questioned, jokingly.

"Uncle Sam," she said without a smile.

I don't think I turned her on. In the end, women are really attracted to guys who have their crap together. I doubt there are many women enamored by the idea of living in a box under a bridge, sucking on a bouillon cube while her man reads Emerson. This is probably not what the old ovaries are pining for. The thing about being irresponsible is it's only cute till you are about twenty-two or so, then it becomes a liability. One day you wake up under a pizza box, the television blaring in your bedroom, the laundry piled up over what might be a bedside table, and you ask yourself, *How did my life get like this? Why don't people like me? Didn't I have a cat and what is that smell?*

———

I WAS LOOKING at the paper today, the cover of the Portland *Tribune*, and they posted thirty mug shots on the front page. There is a big controversy in town about folks getting let out of jail because the city doesn't have enough money to keep them locked up. The whole city is in an uproar—you wouldn't believe it. So I was drinking coffee and staring at these guys, some of them looking like me a few years ago, about twenty-five years old or so, not convict-looking, pretty normal, and if you read what they were in jail for, I could see myself doing the same stupid stuff back in the day. A few of them were driving drunk, a couple got into fights in bars, some of them were caught carrying weapons. The normal criminal fare. And then I got to really seeing the guys, not just looking at them but seeing them. When you truly *see* a person, you start wondering what their life is like and where they grew up and how they got to be the person they have become. I wondered how much they hated being in the paper, because if I were in their shoes there would be some girl somewhere I had a crush on and I would want to disappear because I knew she would see my face. There are certain girls who are attracted to the criminal type, but I have never been attracted to those girls, so it wouldn't help me.

I am not somebody who believes people in prison are worse than I am just because they are in prison. It is true some of our character faults stem from social dynamics, not individual responsibility. What I mean is, the folks in prison or who've made messes of their lives have truly made bad decisions, but what if they have made bad decisions because nobody taught them how to make good decisions? I used to believe the idea that some people are born into great families and get their college paid for, and others are born into poverty and don't get such benefits in life—the rich get richer and the poor get poorer. And this is true, generally. But suppose what is also happening is that the successful get successful because they make good decisions and, far from being a genetic legacy, the art of making good decisions can be learned.

To say it another way, I don't think a guy who is a successful lawyer is that different from a guy in prison. We are all just flesh and bone, just tissue and chemicals. The main difference between the lawyer and somebody in prison is that somewhere along the line, the lawyer learned to make good decisions, open envelopes and pay car insurance, and this sort of thing.

Eighty-five percent of people in prison grew up without a father.

Those of us who grew up without dads, who had mothers taxed by the burden of single parenting, weren't *in school* the day the whole *responsibility* assignment was taught. I don't think there is any other voodoo happening than that. That's the bad news. But before we start throwing bricks through the windows of the children of the Man, we should know that throwing bricks through the window of the children of the Man is a bad decision. It's really that simple. There are bad decisions and good decisions, and if a person makes a string of good decisions, and keeps that string going, he is probably going to be fine. And by that I mean he is probably not going to go to prison for much of anything. Just because we grew up without dads, or life was hard growing up, doesn't mean we have to be complete idiots for the rest of our lives. We can be just as successful as the next guy, as long as we learn a few things. When you think about it, people do it all the time — climb out of the ghetto or whatever, earn a good income, provide for a family, change the direction of their legacy.

The change started for me when I walked out of the IRS office. All of that was my responsibility, I realized. I had put my head in the sand and let life happen to me. I was like a basketball player sitting at center court reading a book, meanwhile the game was happening around me. Reality was happening around me, and reality didn't stop even though I was daydreaming.

But here is the other thing I realized that day. I realized the reason I was burying my head in the sand was not because I hated the Man. The reason I wasn't paying taxes is because I was convinced life was a game I was not invited to play. It has to do with all that belonging stuff I was talking about earlier. I didn't know I could play, and I didn't know I could succeed. I knew in the cognitive sense, the facts told me I could participate, and certainly the flesh on my skeleton testified to the idea I was alive. But I am talking about a very deep realization, a realization that life had been given to me as a gift, a kind of challenge or a game, a bit of a battle, even, an adventure, and God Himself might have been asking me to wake up and take charge.

Taking charge is really about making good decisions. For you and me, it is going to be difficult. Making good decisions is like learning a new language. Some people are born into French homes and they can speak French fluently, and some are born into homes where wisdom rules, and they are going to have a much easier time making good decisions than we are. But we can learn.

My first step was all willpower, which never works. I decided I was going to get my life cleaned up. I bought a little day planner and wrote things in it like *wash the car* and *meet with somebody somewhere*. I was writing these things because staring at the blank pages all the time made me feel like a loser. But it only took a week or two before I noticed I was right back where I started. I would neglect a fifty-dollar payment toward my IRS debt, or I would mouth off at some jerk who rubbed me the wrong way. But that's when I met a man named Salome Thomas-El. Well, I didn't actually meet him, I saw him on television.

I was having trouble sleeping one evening, so I turned on Charlie Rose, who was interviewing this guy Salome Thomas-El. He was a black middle school teacher in Philadelphia, and he had a presence that made you respect him, a soft way with big words and the kind of peace that comes to a man when he has found himself, learned to love himself, and operates for the world out of strength.

Salome had started a chess club in his school, recruiting from the projects around the small campus. He told Charlie Rose what he wanted to teach these students was not how to play chess, necessarily, because chess doesn't really mean anything in the real world, but rather the art of making good decisions. He would walk up to kids hanging around outside a convenience store and ask them if they wanted to learn to play chess. Of course the kids said no, chess not being the most fashionable sport on the playground. So Salome would tell them that telling him no was a *bad* decision, that if somebody offers to teach you something, you should give that person respect, and ask more questions to find out if you might need this information in the future. *That was a bad decision*, Salome said to the kids, *to dismiss me in that way.* The kids didn't really know what to say, so they got tough, threatening him. *Ah,* Salome would say, *another bad decision. I can see that, if you and I were playing chess right now, you would be losing, because in chess, you cannot make bad decisions and win. You have to make good decisions.*

"Have any of you ever played chess?" Salome asked.

"I know how to play chess," one of the kids answered.

"What is the legal move for a Rook?" Salome asked the boy. The boy stood there silently until finally Salome spoke into his shifting eyes, "You are telling a lie, aren't you? You do not know how to play chess. A lie is another bad decision. If you knew how to play chess, you would not make so many bad decisions. You would know, intrinsically, the way to get ahead in life is to make good decisions. And so I will ask you again, and I want you to think about it for five seconds before you answer me. Don't answer right away, because this isn't wise. I want you to think about what I am going to ask you . . .

"Do you want me to teach you how to play chess?"

The children stood there, confused but interested, until one of them blurted out nervously, "Yes, I want to learn chess."

"Fine then. You have made a good decision. This is the first rule of chess. Make good decisions. The only possible way you can lose in chess, and for that matter in life itself, is to make bad decisions. If you do not make bad decisions, you will not lose in chess, or in life. And the more good decisions you make, the better your life will be. It is as easy as that. Who else would like to learn to play chess?" And of course, the kids belonged to Salome from then on, and he has influenced hundreds of children, lined up facing each other, their chess sets placed atop long tables, their hands quick to punch the timers, eight-year-olds, ten-year-olds, teenagers, playing men five times their age and beating them. As Charlie Rose continued the interview, you realized Salome Thomas-El's students are some of the greatest chess players in Philadelphia and they are going off to college, becoming successful, starting families and raising children who feel secure in their homes. These are not the sons of doctors and lawyers, they are kids without fathers. But they learned what their fathers should have taught them. They've learned to make good decisions.

To me it sounded wonderful, that good decisions, that success or whatever you want to call it, was simply about looking at everything like a chess game, that is, you could make good decisions if you wanted—it wasn't about fate. Listening to Thomas-El, I knew I could learn to make good decisions the way a person learns to play the banjo. I sat there and watched the interview, and I believed him. I believed if I made better decisions, I could stay out of trouble, and maybe even build a little life.

After that my friend Curt and I started getting together at this coffee shop to actually play chess. It was just a coincidence that had nothing to do with that interview with Salome, but I was amazed at how much I learned about life from playing the game. We'd play for about two hours, about three games or something, and we did so nearly every day for more than a year, and even though I never actually met Thomas-El and even though he never taught me all the life lessons he teaches the kids in his chess club, lessons came all the same. I actually started applying some of the basics of chess to the basics of life.

Here's what I mean. There were a series of lessons I learned about chess that improved my chances of winning. For example, when I first started, I would line the pieces up, then start making random moves. I rarely lasted more than twenty minutes. But with each lesson, the length of my games increased until eventually I started winning. The first lesson involved having a strategy. Believe it or not, the first fifty times I played, I didn't have a strategy going into the game. And of course I always lost. Curt taught me a few opening moves that would not leave important pieces vulnerable and would set up attacks at the same time. Once I learned these moves, I would move the pieces, not just randomly or in a way that felt wise in the moment, but in line with a kind of overall plan. Now I realize all of this sounds trivial, but this became an important lesson for me in life. It had been a long time since I had sat down and set some goals, really got a vision for what I wanted my life to look like. I wondered if something so simple as spending an hour going through some goals and writing them down in a book could have the same effect in life that it did in chess.

This was about the time my dreams became more passionate about being a published writer. I had been working for a publishing company for a while and began to wonder, seriously, if it was time to make a go at a book of my own. So I sat down and made a list of some things I would need to do in order to get published. I needed a few chapters, I needed an editor I could send the chapters to in order to get feedback, and I needed a list of publishers I could send the book to. So I wrote all of this down, which took about ten minutes, then I decided I was going to do it, that this was my strategy for doing what I really wanted to do with my life. And amazingly, I did it. After writing it down, it just felt like this to-do list is what I was supposed to do with my time. I was supposed to get this list of things done. There wasn't any discipline involved, either. I had written down the plan, so my mind just assumed getting the things on this list done was what I was supposed to do.

I was kind of amazed at how much of my time I had spent wandering around, not really knowing what I was doing or where I was going, only wanting random things in a random universe. I don't know how many months, how many years I spent sitting and watching television, complaining to myself about how boring life was.

It wasn't long after this that I was looking at my first book contract. I smelled it, laid it on the floor and rolled around on it, took it to various coffee shops and set it on the table, hoping people would ask me what sort of legal thing I was looking at. I dropped it on the floor at the grocery store, asking people to excuse me as I picked up my book contract, that sort of thing. It was great. And I don't mean to make it sound like if you sit down and make some goals you are going to get everything you want in life, but I do believe if you don't come up with some kind of strategy you probably never will.

So, I started wondering if there really was something to this *chess teaches boys about life* thing, and I tried to come up with a few more lessons. I think some of them are pretty good.

The second thing I learned had to do with patience. Curt would beat me about half the time because he was very good, but I noticed the times I beat him were the times I didn't rush into anything. That's the thing when you're playing chess: you always see this terrific move, and then you make the move only to find you opened up a world of trouble for yourself. I had to take my time, think things through. I started looking at decisions like paths in the road, wondering where each path was going to take me. I learned not to trust my instincts, seeing that often something that looked like a good move would cost me everything. Sometimes I would even walk away from the table, go to the bathroom or just stretch and rest my head for a second. This annoyed Curt to no end, but if I took my time and didn't react, the percentage chance of my winning increased. On nights when I was patient, I almost always won. But on nights when Curt took more time, of course, he would win.

It sounds too easy, perhaps, you just get up and do some deep knee bends every once in a while and you win, but it isn't that simple. The most difficult temptation, in chess and in life, is the temptation to react. Reacting without thinking never, ever works. As boring as chess sounds, you'd be amazed at how much emotion gets pumping when somebody takes one of your major pieces. On the outside, you're sitting there like an old man, but on the inside you're jumping across the table beating your opponent over the head with a Starbucks thermos.

So that's where patience comes in. I was tempted to react by killing any of my opponent's pieces I could, but those are never good moves. As far as I can tell, the trick is to stick with your strategy, no matter what your emotions are telling you to do. I mean, if a person can do that, they are going to do very well in life, no matter what setbacks they encounter.

I realized I spent much of my time reacting. If somebody offended me, I was quick to react rather than consider what reacting was going to cost me, and whether the price was too much to pay to get revenge. I've found if a guy can control his emotions, he is going to go a great deal further in life. Sometimes that means walking away. And so even in casual conversation with friends, I started being more calculative about what I said and did, being careful not to offend, and if offended, working to bring peace into the situation. The trick is to stick with the plan. If the plan is to finish school and become a doctor, or work hard and move up the company ladder, then throwing somebody through a window would be a departure from the plan.

I used to know this guy named Ben who was always being chosen to lead everything. To be honest, the guy bothered me for the longest time. We'd have coffee and I would ask him a question, kind of enter into debate about some stupid issue, and he would sit there thinking about it then come back with a safe answer, very objective. Like I said, it was annoying. But pretty soon I started noticing most of the guys in our circle respected Ben, really wanted his opinion about things, and the girls all wanted to date him. I realized, also, that what bugged me about him not entering into debate was that I wanted him to stoop to my level, I wanted him to be a reactor. The more patient and calculated Ben was, the more he was asked to lead, and the more respect he got from everybody around him.

And so I started noticing the guys who weren't respected much in life — that is, they weren't close to a group of guys, and girls generally felt uncomfortable around them. They were guys who reacted. They were too loud. They didn't control their body movements. They didn't sound wise when they talked. They would say whatever came into their minds before processing their remarks, filtering them, really thinking about where their comments were going.

I had to swallow my pride on this one. I had to act

more like Ben. It took a lot of practice, to tell you the truth. I have this annoying character flaw in that I always want to be right. Somebody would say something that I disagreed with, and I would open my big mouth and try to correct them, or just make myself sound smart. But people who react never sound smart. It's the people who don't talk who sound smart, the people who don't use a lot of words.

I think there are usually a couple languages being used when two people are having a conversation. The first is whatever words are being spoken, and they say whatever they say. But the other is this hidden language, the emotions that go pumping through a person, trying to get him to do and say things that are going to make him look like an idiot. I might say with my mouth something really wise and practical. But if I were just reacting, that other language would say I wasn't in control, I was weak, insecure. And that's the thing with Ben: he never looked that way. He always came off as thoughtful and reflective and in command of his thoughts and actions. It's no wonder he was always asked to lead.

I'm not saying we should all become politicians. That would be an aggravating universe, to say the least. But I know life got a bit better when I stopped reacting all the time. Because of this, I don't have a bunch of people mad at me.

I heard somebody say that a good idea was to count to five before responding to a threatening situation. At first

I thought this might get confusing, as though we might be tempted to answer every question by whispering the number *six*, but what this person was really doing was teaching people not to react. For me, five was a pretty low number. If we were just talking about baseball or something, that was fine, but if emotions got heated, I would have to count to a million. I would have to politely leave—tell my body to smile and say thanks or whatever, keep on counting, then go home and feel a lot of anger or bitterness or jealousy. But it got easier. After a while, you realize that by walking away, by not getting angry, you are winning, moving ahead, and you get addicted to it. You get used to acting wisely and you like it. You realize this is a better system because it offers you something. It offers you life.

———

BUT I AM leading you on. I am making you believe wisdom is a sure thing. But that isn't true. Wisdom only increases your chances of success. The truth is we aren't always going to win. Life throws stuff at us we can't beat. It happens to everyone. The hardest lesson is learning how to lose. The thing about chess, and about life too, is we are all going to fail. Even if you win a game of chess, it's usually a bloody mess by the end. It stinks in the middle of it, because you lose one piece and you start thinking the game is over. I mean you really feel it, your mind gets all dark and you start believing you are a loser, and you feel like quitting. You wonder how you got yourself into this mess, and your clouded judgment can't see a way out. I've lost a lot of chess games well before a game was over. I start seeing myself losing, imagining myself losing. But I noticed one time that, even after I had lost a major piece, I somehow managed to win the game. In a way, that game broke a trend. And the next time I got myself into that situation, I wondered if there was still a chance, and so I stayed in the game. I stayed with a strategy and took my time, and, well, I won more games that way.

It happens in life too. I can't list the number of times I thought life was completely over, that I had ruined everything and was going to end up living in a box under a bridge. There was the Christmas morning, when I was a kid, I shot out the rear window of my neighbor's truck with my new BB gun, the time I spilled a half-gallon of red paint on the new living room carpet, the time I stepped on my first girlfriend's pet turtle. Those were awful days, to be sure, but looking back I'm slightly amused at the idea I thought I had ruined everything. It was just paint, just glass, just, um, a turtle.

Sometimes I wish I could go back in time, sit down with myself and explain things were going to be okay, that everybody loses ground sometimes and it doesn't mean anything. It's the way life works. This is hard to understand in the moment. You get to thinking about the girl who rejected you, the job you got fired from, the test you failed, and you lose sight of the big picture—the fact that life has a beautiful way of remaking itself every few weeks. The things that matter right now aren't going to matter a month from now, a year from now.

I believe there is something called wisdom. John MacMurray would point me to the book of Proverbs, which contains the brief, Polaroid snapshots of Solomon, one of the wisest men who ever lived. They're just short little sayings, like the ones you crack open in fortune cookies, and they can be found right around the middle of your Bible. I wanted to start making good decisions, and overheard John saying to somebody this was a good place to start for basic life wisdom. I started reading a chapter every morning, or every evening before I went to bed. You wouldn't believe how often the verses come back to you when you are just doing everyday things. I think if you read Proverbs, or the Bible in general, your percentage chance of success goes through the roof. Two thousand years of tested wisdom can't steer you wrong. If you really want to learn to make better decisions, the book of Proverbs is a good place to start.

Like I said, none of us is going to get it perfect, but you have to figure, a guy who goes into his life with a bit of strategy, and a whole lot of patience, and doesn't give up when he fails, is going to be fine. It works for Salome Thomas-El's kids, and I think it will work for us too.

Chapter Nine

GIRLS:
THE THING TONY SAID

Here is a story that is true . . .

A week ago, I went to a coffee shop in southeast Portland, on Ankeny, and happened to notice a pretty girl sitting outside the shop talking to someone who looked to be her boyfriend. I went in and ordered coffee, sat down, and started checking my e-mail—diddling around, not wanting to get started writing. The girl and the boy were outside the window next to me, and he was looking across the street at a Mexican restaurant, at the mural of a cucumber wearing a cowboy hat. And you could see in the boy's expression he was looking at the mural but not thinking about it, only wanting the girl to think he was thinking about it, and you could see in his expression he was trying to hold himself together.

The guy stood, and she stood, and she came toward him, and he wrapped her up, holding her for a minute until she motioned out of it. She slowly made a circle on his back with her palm, and he walked away with his head down, fumbling for his keys.

I knew then that this had been a breakup. A rejection. I knew because it happened to me once before. Maybe even twice, or fifty-seven times, I've lost track.

Then the girl came into the coffee shop to gather her things, only to be recognized by another man, whom she looked at with a smile, a friendly and inviting smile. He stood there talking to her for a minute, nervous about the conversation, and she helped him by reaching out and touching his arm, tilting her head to the side and shyly laughing, then reaching out and touching his arm again. He asked her something, and she nodded, and he walked over and picked up a pen off the counter, writing her phone number on a napkin. She smiled at him again and they began walking toward the door. I wondered at how funny it was that she was flirting with another guy just after rejecting the one outside.

Then the girl noticed a friend sitting at the table next to me, this time a girl. They hugged like old friends, then sat down and started talking. The second boy stood by the door for a minute until he realized he was forgotten, then tried to walk away without being noticed.

I know he was trying to walk away without being noticed because that had happened to me too. Once or maybe twice, or fifty-seven times.

The two girls sat down, and I could hear them talking. The first girl explained she hoped her boyfriend at the table outside wasn't hurt too much, and the other girl pursed her lips and lifted her eyebrows. And then the girl said she liked to flirt—that she just liked it—and that she was always getting herself in a bind.

"Boys *like* you," the friend said, and tilted her head to smile again.

After a while I felt guilty for listening, and I wasn't getting any work done, so I loaded my laptop into my bag, cleared my table, and went home. That afternoon, I wondered about girls, about how much they want to feel pretty and wanted, and how there were times the boy who was affirming them didn't mean very much.

A few hours at home had the lawn mowed, so I showered and decided to go to a different coffee shop to try again at writing. I drove to a place called Palio, ordered some tea, then opened my computer to check my e-mail and diddle. After ten minutes passed, to my surprise the girl came in—the same girl from the coffee shop on Ankeny. She was with a different guy, not the guy who took down her number, and not the first guy she sat with at the table outside, but a fully different guy. They had a conversation about who would pay for the pastries, and he didn't have any money that day. So, she paid, and they took their plates and crossed the street onto a circle of lawn, in the center behind a perimeter of shrubs.

After twenty minutes, I got lost in some correspondence but was awakened by the slow-moving figure of her date, standing at the curb of the lawn alone, looking down at the street and fidgeting in his pocket for his keys, pulling them out and thumbing through them, trying to find the one that starts the car. He crossed the street as though there were a thousand people watching, his motion careful and rigid. The girl came around the shrubs, carrying two plates, looking across toward the coffee shop with some regret — some pleasure, but some regret.

I wrote a little that day and then went home, feeling somewhat privileged and lucky I had seen a girl break up with two guys in one day. I say privileged because it is a great story, and lucky because I hadn't been one of the guys.

———

AND THIS IS the part of the story where I tell you what it is a girl really wants from a guy, what it is that stops her looking and has her fascinated with a particular boy, you or me, for example. But the truth is I don't know. I really don't.

I know some guys turn girls on and some guys don't. I know some girls play games and some girls don't. I also know it feels good to be tired of it. I only say that because there was a day when I would be attracted to a particular girl and yet the attraction would have nothing to do with her. What I mean is, I would be attracted to a girl, and feel very real feelings for her, only because she was a challenge and I wanted to know whether I had what it took to be the one she would end up dating. Most of the time I wasn't, and worse, if I was, I lost interest shortly after she became attracted. I guess that's why they call it a game.

Watching the woman at the coffee shop made me realize how shallow the game was, and that my soul was more than a bit tired of it. For the first time, perhaps, I didn't want to play anymore. I wanted something else, something better.

I learned to put words to what I wanted from my friend Tony. We were having dinner at a Mexican place a while back and I had just started seeing a girl. I was telling Tony how much I liked her, how I liked her honesty and the feeling I got when I was with her. I liked that she was a girl I wasn't uncomfortable praying with, and this was something different from past relationships. Tony said he thought she sounded great. But then he asked if I thought I deserved to be in a relationship at all.

"I don't know," I told him. "What do you mean?"

"Do you feel a girl would be grateful to have you in her life?" he asked.

"I've never thought about it," I told him. In relationships, I had spent most of my time wondering if the girl liked me, and moreover, if I was likeable. I think Tony was asking a different question.

"What are you getting at?" I asked.

"I don't know," Tony said. "It's just that with my wife, with Aimee, I've come to the conclusion I don't deserve her. I really don't. And the fact she would want to spend the rest of her life with me strikes me as incredible. I'm grateful, is all I am saying."

"Do you think I'm not grateful?" I asked my friend.

"Not saying that," Tony stated. "Just saying that I think we can use other people, romantic stuff, to validate ourselves. It has nothing to do with love. And when you find love, or when you are mature enough to understand it, the feeling you get is gratitude. I'm not saying I am mature by any means," Tony continued, "but when I wake up in the morning and look at my wife sleeping next to me, I am sometimes overcome that another human being would want to share her life with me."

The thing Tony said stuck with me. And I've started to wonder if what I was really lacking in my understanding of relationships was humility. I don't mean to sound mushy or weak, because that will kill a relationship too, but I wondered if love stemming from the ego and love stemming from the heart were very different things, and what was happening in my soul was a kind of transition from immaturity to maturity.

Chapter Ten

SEX:
THE VALUE OF THE DOLLAR IN ARGENTINA

A few weeks ago I was at the University of Texas. Some guys asked me to come to their fraternity house to have a talk, just a lot of us sitting around in the middle of the night. There was going to be about fifty of them or so, and they wanted to talk about faith and morality. We left campus pretty late, weaving through side streets, past an outdoor bar spilling with students standing awkwardly next to each other, dressed for mating, cackling like birds. The fraternity house was a multimillion dollar limestone and cedar complex with a restaurant kitchen and dining area, ten-foot high fireplaces and leather chairs, couches sunk into a polished concrete pit surrounded by a gallery of black-and-white photographs; the watchful eye of fraternity fathers, fifties Longhorns holding football trophies, bottles of beer, their women standing behind them all lipstick and teeth, hair pinned back like nurses at Pearl Harbor.

"In the bathroom of this place there's a stack of porn with *Blue Like Jazz* sitting on top," one of the guys said to me as I walked in the house. The guy was the son of an oil tycoon, a sort-of Christian. He said this not smiling, just stating a fact, letting me know who I was about to talk to.

He led me through the dining area, through some heavy double doors into the room with the pit of leather couches, young men already seated, quiet, fidgety, not sure they wanted to be there or why, as though meeting to talk about spirituality was akin to talking about *Star Trek*. They all got up and shook my hand, about fifty of them. They leaned in like their fathers taught them. They looked me in the eye, *glad you are here, good to see you, thanks for coming, liked your book, glad to have you at Texas*, all that.

"There's a bar full of women down the street," I said, thumbing toward the window as I sat down.

"Dollar beer night," one of them nodded.

"Why aren't you there?" I asked.

"They do it every week," somebody said.

"So, you want to talk about faith, about God," I stated, almost as a question. Nobody answered for a minute.

"It's not easy," one of them finally said.

"Being a Christian?" I asked.

"Right," he confirmed.

"Unless you live in the suburbs and surround yourself with Christians who validate your identity, following Jesus is going to be difficult. You haven't chosen to do that." As I said this, it seemed to let some of the stiff air out of the room.

"You think it's okay to live here?" another asked.

"I think it's wrong to run and hide. I don't know if it's right for you to live here. That is different for every person."

"There's not a lot of morality around here," one of the guys spoke up. "I mean it's a good-old-boy faith, you know. You're a Christian because every good Republican is a Christian. But . . ." This kid was fidgeting a bit; he slid down a little in his chair.

"But what?" I asked.

"But," he said, as a statement, shrugging his shoulders.

"But beer? But women?" I asked, finishing his comments.

"But women," another of them clarified, dismissing the beer as a minor problem.

"What is the thing with women around here?" I asked.

"It's difficult, you know. You're weak if you don't sleep around. The Mayberry act doesn't get you far."

"I see," I said.

"They're kind of everywhere. You've been around campus."

"I have. They are everywhere, that is for sure."

"Right," one of the guys on the couch leaned in. "And I

really like them. I mean, you know, I really like it." When he said *it* some of the guys laughed. I nodded my head. "I'm not saying it's right," he continued. "I'm just saying, I like it. I like sex. Do you think I am going to go to hell or something?"

"I don't think having sex is the way you get to hell. Heaven and hell are about who you know, not what you do. *Who you know saves you from what you did and who you are inside.* I'm not saying that gives us license to go have sex anytime we want with any woman we want. Morality is more important and more beneficial than any of us know. But heaven and hell are something different."

"It's wrong, though," one of the guys said, almost as a question.

"Yeah, I think it's wrong," I started in. "But let's not turn the idea of right and wrong into coloring book material. This is a very complex subject. Sin, if we want to call it sin, is stuff that we do that God doesn't like, and the reason He doesn't like it is because He loves us, He is fathering us, and when we sin, we weaken ourselves, we confuse ourselves, we practice immaturity. He doesn't like that, not because He wants to feel powerful or right, but because He wants what is best for us. That's the first thing we have to remember about all of this."

"Sex doesn't feel wrong," one of the guys said, leaning forward a bit, being slightly sarcastic but also honest.

"Okay," I said. "Let me explain it another way. You guys are all Republicans, right?" Most of the guys nodded their heads *yes*. "Well, let's consider the value of the dollar.

Ultimately, logically, the dollar has no value at all. It's a piece of paper. It only has value because we say it has value, and because we agree on a system of bartering that maintains that value. Great care is taken to keep the value of the dollar strong. Smart guys in Washington and New York lose sleep over this. And we all watched what happened in Argentina a few years ago. We watched what happened when the value of a currency declined rapidly. It's not a good thing. Sex is like that. God is concerned with the value of sex staying high. It's important to a person's health, a family's health, and a society's health. But like anything, sex can be cheapened in our minds, so we don't hold it in high esteem. God doesn't think this is a good thing. Stuff God doesn't think is good is called sin."

"What happens when sex is cheapened?" somebody asked.

"A lot happens. The main thing is there is no sacred physical territory associated with commitment. There can still be emotional territory, but there isn't anything physical, experiential, that a man and a woman have only with each other. Sleeping around does something to the heart, to the mind. It leaves less commodity to spend on a sacred mate. But all of that sounds pretty fluffy. Let me break it down into practical stuff. Women saying no to men, not letting men have sex with them, causes men to step up. If, in order to have sex with them, women demanded you got a job and shaved every day and didn't dress like a dork or sit around playing video games, then all of us would do just that. We all want to have sex, right?"

"Amen," one of the guys said, which drew some laughter.

"So if a woman demanded that you acted like a gentleman," I continued, "that you were able to commit and focus, then everybody in this room would do just that, if for no other reason than we want to have sex. And this in turn would be good for families, would be good for communities. Let's face it, we're guys, and too often we are going to take the path of least resistance. Many of us are the way we are because women are attracted to a certain kind of man. We may not have realized this dynamic was shaping us, but it has been. Nobody is exempt. So, when sex gets cheapened, we are getting what we want without having to pay for it. That's not good for anybody, not in the long run anyway. It's a great system, you know."

"But women don't withhold sex. It doesn't work like that any more," a guy from the back of the room stated.

"That's true," I said. "Women are imitating men, I think. The presupposition is that men are right, and in order for a woman to be successful, she should not act like a woman but like a man. Thanks for the compliment, but I disagree. I think men need women to be women, and we need to be made to jump through some hoops. If a woman withholds sex until she gets what *she* wants, we are all better for it."

There was some silence after I said this. Some of the

guys were thinking about it, some of them I could tell were disagreeing.

"You know," I started in, softly, "I hate this as much as you guys do. You try to take away people's sex, try to make people feel guilty or something, and everybody hates you for it. I mean you're a geek, right? And I don't want to be that guy. I really don't. It's just that my dad left my mom when I was a kid, and I remember visiting him and he always had some girl living with him, or was sleeping around with a girl half his age, and that affected me. I think my dad just thought it didn't matter, that he should be able to sleep with whomever he wanted. But what I needed him to do was stay with my mom, love my mother and be my father. I think we can think nobody is affected by our actions, by our habits, but they are. We aren't independent creatures, you know. We are all connected. And in a family, in marriage, it's important that sex be something special, and as men, it's important we take the initiative in protecting it. Those habits start now. Greg Spencer, a professor friend of mine, would say sex is the most psychologically involving of the physical acts. Men fantasize that sex is mere biology. Yet nothing seems to affect us quite as deeply as sex when it is abused. I hope you don't fault me for saying all of this."

"I think you make a good point," one of the guys said, crossing his legs and looking around the room at the rest of the guys. "But I think the thing all of us are dealing with is we are in this environment where we are going to be unfashionable unless we are routinely having sex and telling stories about it. Unless we are using women. That is the issue. And it's a powerful thing. None of us wants to be the guy who doesn't do that. I hear you, Don," and he looked at me as he said this, "but the desire to not be marginalized may be stronger than the desire for sex. In other words, I would rather sleep around, get some pleasure, whatever, and not look bad in front of my brothers."

"Yeah, I understand," I said. "That's honest. Like I said, it's hard, you know, you are faced with certain challenges being a Christian in this environment. And you aren't always going to do well. But let's look at this another way. Let's say you had a friend who was forty years old, and let's say this guy played video games all night, slept around with ten different women, whoever he could get to have sex with him, drank all the time, partied it up, the whole bit. Would you respect that guy?" The group shook their heads no, some of them voicing that they would think of him as a loser.

"Why?" I asked. "Why would this guy be a loser?"

"Because he's forty," somebody spoke up.

"What does that have to do with it? If somebody in your fraternity lives like this, he's not a loser. Apparently, he is well-esteemed."

The group said that it was different because the other guy is supposed to be mature. He's supposed to have his life together.

"Yeah, I think so," I began. "I think he is supposed to

be mature, because he is forty. But we've kind of said something here, haven't we? We've said maturity doesn't stay up all night playing video games and doesn't sleep with ten women. Maturity practices self-discipline, and points a person's character toward a noble aim. And I think, even in your early twenties, there is this need for guys like us to grow up, to sort of usher other boys into manhood, into commitment, into self-respect and an understanding that actions matter to more people than just ourselves. Think of yourselves as prophets if you want. You're making a statement with the way you live your life. You're passing guys up, you are beating them to maturity. And there isn't any better way to help somebody than to have the boldness to pass them up. It makes them feel the pressure to mature themselves. I'm not saying this to be a wet blanket, you know. That's not what I mean. None of us have the right to judge our brothers. If you act mature, and don't judge others, you will be respected. I really think that is true."

The group and I talked till late into the night, talked more about sex, about spirituality, about the need for men, strong and good men, and how the world had emasculated us, turning us into thoughtless apes. Even as we talked, I felt the things we were saying were true, that women needed us to become strong, to be committed and control our desires for sex so they were used to affirm exclusive unity, love, and family.

I won't lie to you. I've found myself wondering at times

whether protecting the value of sex is all that important. Physical desire has a way of shaping a person's philosophy. But in the end I can't turn a blind eye to those who say restraint is a good idea. It's true most people who make those statements don't make them well, or winsomely, and come off sounding anything but revolutionary, but underneath it all, the idea has merit. As a Christian, I know I need God to deliver me from a warped view of sex.

Not long ago I rented the movie *Kinsey*, a film about Dr. Alfred Kinsey, a former professor of entomology and zoology at Indiana University. Kinsey caught hell when he created the Kinsey Institute for Research in Sex, Gender, and Reproduction, which greatly increased the degree of honesty with which people discussed their sexual tendencies and habits. His research and finding is charged with the advent of the sexual revolution in the sixties.

Kinsey's methodology mostly involved interviewing people in anonymity, using coding procedures so the greatest honesty could be insured. His findings were mildly controversial, setting the sexual instinct a bit more in the animal category than conservatives felt comfortable admitting. As his research continued, however, Kinsey's methodology grew more compulsive until he encouraged his staff members to have sex with each other's wives, and he himself seduced a fellow male staff member. The thing became something of a controlled orgy, and as the film depicts this slide, much of the mental sobriety and focus of the characters gets distorted. Staff workers were jealous of each other, wives felt confused, Kinsey's research lacked point. In the end, Kinsey realized sex cannot be removed from love, that the strictly physical cannot be understood in isolation from the poetic or romantic, that, in fact, animal behavior must be tempered by morality stemming from something spiritual.

I thought of Kinsey's revelation again and wondered if some of the more traditional views on sex could not, at least to some degree, be supported by the very researcher the traditionalists have come to hate.

The great argument, then, is not whether sex is good or bad outside a relational commitment, but whether sex is *for* anything other than the release of pleasure. There is no scientific evidence to suggest sex is *for* bonding. Common sense tells us sex bonds people, but science can't go into the poetic. The tendency, when pleasure drives logic, is to reduce sex to a dry Darwinian definition, ignoring the poetry of our bodies. And this doesn't sound like much of a crime, until we remember the argument about the value of the dollar. Poetics, then, matter. What we feel about something, what we agree about for the sake of health and progress becomes critical. I think of sex this way, not only because this is the way God thinks about sex, but because logically, even apart from some sort of Christian morality, the poetic interpretation has to be upheld.

Chapter Eleven

INTEGRITY:
HOW TO PAY FOR A FREE CELL PHONE

The first and foremost rule in the MacMurray home, and I've personally observed this, is *always tell the truth*. John says it's the basis for all healthy relationships. Trust can't exist without this rule working. Which reminds me of a story . . . John and I were sitting in the family room one night watching Sports Center when he asked about my new cell phone. I had set it down on the armrest, and he picked it up, wondering out loud at how small it was.

"I got it free," I told him.

"How did you get it for free?" he asked.

"Well, my other one broke, so I took it in to see if they

could replace it. They had this new computer system at the Sprint store downtown, and they didn't have their records. They didn't know whether mine was still under warranty. It wasn't, I knew, because I had looked at the receipt before I brought it in. It was more than a year old. The guy asked me about it, and I told him I didn't know, but it was right around a year. Just a white lie, you know. Anyway, the phone was so messed up they replaced it with the newer model. So, I got a free phone."

John kept looking at the phone for a minute, then handed it back to me and went into the kitchen to get an apple. He came back and sat down, and we talked about the Seahawks for a while, wondering between ourselves if Holmgren could get them to the Superbowl.

"Did you ever see that movie *The Family Man* with Nicolas Cage?" John asked while taking a bite of his apple, leaving the conversation about football.

"I think I did see it, yeah. It's like *Scrooge* or something, right?" I asked.

"Something like that," John continued. "There's this scene in the movie where Nicolas Cage walks into a convenience store to get a cup of coffee or something, I don't remember. And Don Cheadle plays the guy working at the counter. Turns out there's a girl in line before Nicolas Cage, and she is buying something for ninety-nine cents, and she hands Cheadle a dollar. Cheadle takes nine dollars out of the till and counts it out to the girl, giving her way too much change, right?"

"Right," I say.

"And the girl doesn't correct him. She sees that he is handing her way too much money—change for a ten—yet she picks it up and puts it in her pocket without saying a word. And as she is walking out the door, Cheadle stops her, you know, to give her another chance. He asks her if there is anything else she needs. She shakes her head *no* and walks out."

"I see what you're getting at, John," I say, knowing he is trying to make me feel guilty about the phone.

"Let me finish," he says. "So Cheadle looks over at Nicolas Cage, and he says, *Did you see that? She was willing to sell her character for nine dollars. Nine dollars!*" After John says this, he looks back at the television. He picks up the remote and turns up the volume. After a little while I speak up.

"Do you think that is what I am doing?" I asked. ". . . with the phone and all? Do you think I am selling my character or something?" And to be honest, I said this with a smirk.

"I do," John said, not being judgmental, just stating a fact. "I don't mean to be a holy roller, Don," he continued, "but the Bible talks about having a calloused heart. That's when sin, after a period of time, has so deceived us we no longer care whether our thoughts and actions are right or wrong. And we have to guard against that. Our hearts will go there easily, and often over what looks like little things—little white lies. All I am saying to you, as your friend, is, Watch for this kind of thing."

"I see," I told him. We didn't talk about it after that. We talked more about the Seahawks, then about an old rerun of *The X-Files* that came on. John went to bed soon after that, and I surfed the channels and watched an interview with Richard Nixon from back in the day. He looked tired. This was after all the Watergate stuff. He looked tired but also relatively innocent. I am not saying he didn't do anything wrong, I just mean by today's standards, he looked innocent. Basically, he cheated to get ahead in politics. That's hardly a crime today. It's almost like people don't even respect a politician who can't get away with distorting the truth. I didn't like that he looked so innocent. And I wondered why he didn't just admit he did something wrong. I went back to the Sprint store the next day. It cost me more than nine dollars, but I got my character back.

Chapter Twelve

WORK ETHIC:
HOW THE CHINESE DO WAR

During the years I lived with the MacMurrays, I discovered children were loud. In the mornings they rise with the sun and get into the cereal before their parents wake. Within ten minutes, one of them has stabbed the other with a fork and so you rouse each morning to the sounds of murder. If you place a pillow over your head or keep a fan running, you can ignore it for ten minutes or so, but sooner or later you have to go downstairs to lock the screaming one in the pantry.

When Chris was three or so, and Elle was a year and a half, both of them would get up early as farmers, even though they didn't have jobs. I slept late because after you see the sun rise over Mount Hood a couple times, you get over it and realize you don't have to *see* something beautiful to make it beautiful. It's beautiful whether you see it or not. So, after experiencing the morning ritual a few times, I decided to go back to my old ways of sleeping. The morning sacrament was a nice place to visit, but dreamland is where I belonged.

I say this because there aren't many pleasures I enjoy more than sleep. I sleep till I am done, normally, and haven't set an alarm in years. I'm not lazy, mind you, I just find it odd anybody would program a machine to wake them. God made the brain so it would wake on its own, and as a follower of Jesus, I am a strict adherent to His system. Call me a fundamentalist if you want.

The awful truth about living with a family, however, is you don't get a lot of sleep. Unless you can afford a nanny or send your toddler to military school, which is what I intend to do, you are going to get up with the sun. There is nothing you can do about it. I tried to get around this fact, but after discovering I was using white noise and pillows to ignore the chaos of morning, Chris decided to start climbing the stairs to wake me in person. He would stand at the foot of my bed and stare at me, making me feel I was some kind of animal living in his house. I would tell him the guilt wasn't working, that I was a grown man and could sleep as long as I wanted, but he would continue staring, using all sorts of three-year-old silent tactics he probably learned from a book about how the Chinese do war.

"What do you want, Chris?" I would say into my pillow, my breath smelling like a litterbox.

"You sleeping?" Chris would ask, pulling his thumb out of his mouth.

"I am sleeping. When Don lies down and doesn't move, he is sleeping."

"Dad says you sleep all the time and never stop."

"But I'm not sleeping anymore, am I, Chris?"

And about this time Elle, who was slow when it came to climbing stairs, would summit the top step to laugh and gasp, then roll onto my bed to poke her finger in my ear before she and Chris would jump on my head. Something else they probably learned from the Samurai.

I would push them off but they would come again and no amount of pushing or kicking could get them to leave. I tried everything. I faked my death, gasping as though I couldn't get air, rolling off the bed, mumbling about being allergic to children. I slept in various Halloween costumes — ghosts, axe murderers, Raggedy Andy. But nothing worked. They would come, morning after morning, consistent and unfailing, like little droplets of water dripped upon my forehead.

After twenty minutes of this, Chris would get bored or hungry and leave. This was hardly a relief, however, as Elle had yet to develop the courage to navigate the *down* direction of the stairs. She would stand at the top of the steps, face my direction, and let out the sort of scream a small town could employ to warn people of tornados. One found it hard to believe such a small creature (four appendages and a head coming out of a pudgy diaper) could make such a loud noise.

"Scoot down on your butt, Elle," I would say into my mattress, my lips hardly parting under the weight of my own head. And in response she would warn me of tornados.

"Roll! Grip a pillow and roll," I would say, offering her one of my pillows.

She would gasp, cry again, all the while big crystal tears dove from her plump red cheeks, her arms outstretched in a request for me to carry her, the whole girl routine happening in miniature.

"Elbow. It's nine in the morning, for crying out loud. And a Thursday. Nobody gets up this early on a Thursday." She would stop screaming then, only panting, trying to find a breath through the hiccup-like convulsions of tiny toddler lungs. And with this I would crawl out of bed, lean down to pick her up, and take her downstairs and into the kitchen. After a few seconds, her panting would quiet to awkward breathing, and she would slip her head into my neck, and then wrap her tiny arms around my shoulders, and of course she had me.

That is the thing with kids, isn't it? I believe God made them small and cute so we wouldn't forget to feed them.

———

"THIS ONE GOT out of its cage," I said to Terri one morning, bringing Elle into the kitchen and setting her on the counter.

"Did you go see Uncle Don this morning, Elbow?" Terri asked, leaning in to kiss Elle on the forehead while stirring a bowl of egg yokes. Elle nodded her head to say yes, her tears still wet on her cheeks, her breathing still post-trauma.

"Did you wake him up like I told you to, Elle?" John commented, coming over from the table, setting the newspaper on the counter.

"So you're the one sending the kids up?" I asked, genuinely curious as to whether John was interrupting my religious freedom.

"Don, it's 9 a.m. I just can't stand it. How can you sleep this late?" he asked, looking at his wife and shaking his head, as though to ask her for an agreement.

"I'm staying out of it," Terri said, still stirring her eggs.

"I'm telling you, Don," John started in. "Enjoy it. Enjoy it while you are young and single. Sooner or later, reality is going to hit you, man, and you won't be sleeping in till noon. That's for sure."

"I get work done," I defended.

"You're a writer, Don. That isn't work. And let's be honest. You write every few days. The rest of the time you goof off, right?" John was being half serious now. And I was taking it a little personally, if you want to know the truth.

"Writing is like that. It's creative work," I said to him.

"You just can't write every day."

"Sure you can," he said. "I've written term papers, I know about writing. You can write if you're not in the mood to write. You're just letting your feelings take over. It's all just work."

———

ABOUT THIS TIME, John and I started hanging out a little more, going on trips to get photos of mountains and sunsets and other free entertainments. The thing is, John is a hard worker. When taking pictures, he gets up early and heads into the elements well before the sun. When you are a nature photographer, there are two windows of time when it's best to take photos: sunrise and sunset. So John, who is notorious for staying up till two in the morning, would often drag himself out of bed at four to drive a couple hours to a trailhead, then hike a couple miles into the mountains to set up for a shot of light coming through trees or first light on mountains. And these were the easy trips. The hard trips had him getting on planes and flying for hours into the middle of nowhere, then hiking for days into a remote wilderness, or having a helicopter drop him off on a mountain peak in New Zealand, all for the hope of some sunset light happening a certain way on a mountain lake, or mist settling low on a valley floor, or a cheetah eating a porcupine, or whatever else nature does. And John would be quick to say nature photography is the easier of his jobs. Running a business, teaching classes, and keeping Terri attracted to him require even more attention than shooting sunsets.

What I am saying is the guy worked hard, and because of this, I learned a bit about work ethic. I learned, for example, a person could enjoy working, rather than experience it as a punishment. John and I talked about it when I went with him to take a picture in the Columbia River Gorge.

We had hiked to the top of a smaller mountain to get a view of Mount Adams, across the river. It had taken us a while to get there, and I was breathing pretty hard at the top, and once there, John looked out at the mountain, then up at the sky and wondered out loud if the evening sun was going to break the clouds.

"It's a great view regardless," I said.

"But it's not worth taking a picture of. Not yet," John told me.

"What are you talking about? It's unbelievable, man."

"Don, there are a million shots like this. Anybody could hike up here on any day and take this shot. We're looking for something a little more exceptional."

"I see," I said, but inside I thought the picture would be fine regardless.

John pulled his twenty-pound tripod out of his backpack and set it up. Then he carefully pulled out his four-by-five camera. It's an old-looking camera you might imagine a guy using in the forties, as though he should have had a big stick in his free hand that would burst in a flash of sparks as he clicked the shot. He unwrapped the camera from some towels and set it atop the tripod, screwing the bottom of the camera to the top of the legs. He looked through the large opening, watching the clouds to see if any light was going to shine through. I went around and looked into the opening and saw Mount Adams in the distance, upside down in the sight of the camera, and the wide Columbia River wandering east, out toward farmland where it would eventually turn north toward Canada. I sat on a rock and watched the stretched-cotton clouds snag across the jagged spine of Mount Adams. I turned further north to see Mount St. Helens, and then Mount Hood to the east and Jefferson directly south, and I watched as a boat in the distance worked up the Columbia toward Cascade Locks. And in all this silence and stillness and beauty John began to unscrew the camera from the tripod. He wasn't going to take the picture.

"What are you doing?" I asked.

"The light isn't right," he said, setting the camera back into the towels and slipping it into the womb of his backpack.

"It's beautiful," I said.

"It is beautiful," he agreed, collapsing the tripod slowly, looking out at the mountain. "But it isn't right."

"Shoot it," I said. "We came all this way."

"We didn't come that far," he said. "And the light isn't

right. I was hoping the sun would break through a little bit and put some color on the glaciers, but it isn't going to happen. High clouds are too thick tonight." And with that, he slid the tripod back into his backpack and loaded the weight onto his shoulders. "You want to look at it anymore or you want to head home?"

"We did come all this way," I said to him.

"I do have a family waiting for me back home," he reminded me.

"Okay," I said, putting my hands in my pockets and turning to take one last look at each of the peaks. John laughed a knowing laugh at me under his breath.

"Getting it all in?" he asked.

"Well, I feel like we should have a moment of silence, you know. Something to respect the mountains."

"The mountains are piles of dirt, Don. Respect God."

"Well, maybe a moment of silence for God, then," I said to him.

"Fine." And John stood there for a second, kind of looking at the ground. Then he looked up at me and said, "You know, I do this all the time. I really love God and all, but why don't we head back home. God made my family, too."

"Right. Well, you've seen one mountain, you've seen them all," I stated, sarcastically.

"Exactly," John said, lowering a foot down the steep steps of the trail.

I took one last look at Adams, and let my eye glide

upriver a bit, noting a waterfall happening in the distance on the northern shore. Then I turned and followed John down the trail. We didn't talk much on the hike back to the parking lot, but I do remember having a new respect for John, and I wondered how often it was that he made these hikes, sometimes ten miles or more, without getting a shot.

"How often does this happen?" I asked as we wound down the mountain in the truck.

"How often does what happen?"

"How often do you do all this work and not get a shot?"

"I don't know. I try not to think about it."

"Just guess," I persisted.

"It happens a great deal," he said. "I don't know, maybe I will use about 10 percent of the shots I take. Maybe a little more."

"Ninety percent of your work gets thrown away?" I asked rhetorically.

"Maybe less than that. I don't know."

"How do you do it, John? I mean how do you get out of bed at four in the morning or hike up into the mountains for days without knowing you are going to get a shot. Doesn't that drive you nuts, knowing the chances of your getting a good picture are so low?"

"But that isn't the way you are supposed to think about work, Don. It isn't about what you don't get done; it's about what you do get done. The price of one good shot is nine other hikes, nine other times I have to get out of bed. That's the cost of a great moment."

"You make pretty good money at this?" I asked.

"I make a lot of money, if that is what you are asking."

"How much money do you make?" I asked.

"None of your business," he said.

"A million?" I asked.

"What are you, my banker?" he chortled.

John continued to wind down the mountain, his headlights coming on to sweep through forest that seemed to grow denser the lower we descended.

"It's cool, you know. You get to do what you want and make money at it. And a lot of money, too. How many people can say that?" I asked.

"It's a blessing," John said. "But, you get to do what you want, too. You get to write books and all."

"Yeah, but I don't make any money at it."

"You think I always made money doing this? Ask Terri, Don. I ate a lot of peanut butter in the early years. In fact, for several years, we had very little. God *always* provided for our needs, but I remember when Terri and I were dating she would feed me dinner probably six out of seven nights. And if it weren't for her, I would never have seen a movie or gone for a meal. She was always paying for our meals. It was more than a little humiliating. She was so cool though. She would never make me feel that way, only encourage me about what great photos I was getting. Terri has always had it together, man. I was just some dope with a camera."

"Terri bought you dinners when you were dating!" I said, laughing to myself.

"Hey, that's how it is when you're trying to get started. It's the starving artist thing, you know."

"That's the cost of pursuing your dream, you mean."

"What are you, some kind of Hallmark card, now?" He laughed cynically.

"You're the one who lived off your woman," I said under my breath. We were quiet for a few minutes. Then, I confessed to John I didn't like to work. And I didn't understand why we had to.

"It's a crazy system," I started in. "God created us so we had to eat and drink, and he created the earth so we have to work to get food and water, so that means God created us so we have to work. It kind of stinks. It's all about original sin or something, isn't it?"

"No," John stated, putting on his theologian hat. "It isn't. Adam and Eve had to work before the Fall. Work isn't punishment, it's reward."

"How is it reward?" I asked.

"Well, that's the obvious question. And the answer is going to sound cheesy, but hear me out. It's about God," he said.

"God. So I should work because God wants me to work. So it's a guilt thing."

"No, not at all. Guilt should not be a motivation. Work

exists for a lot of reasons. God worked. He created the earth and the cosmos. We work to participate in the God-life, to imitate God. That's also why we take a Sabbath. Work is one of the ways we engage in life, one of the ways we participate. It's important. The Bible says that whatever we do, whatever work we do, we do it unto the Lord, to please Him. Just like I do the things I know honor or please Terri."

"So, I get up in the morning and do work for God."

"Right. If you work for yourself, you are going to be let down, or you are going to work too much because I am trying to redeem myself or something, or you are going to be lazy. God is the only motivation I have found where the law of diminishing returns doesn't apply. I get joy in knowing Him, and He makes sense of my life, my family, my money, my work. And work is just a tool. It is the means to a good end, not the end itself."

"So, I could work a jackhammer and it wouldn't matter."

"Working a jackhammer is a noble profession," John said. "That's the thing that gets to me, you know, because people think if they are somebody who does some kind of sexy work, they are more valuable. It's not true. All work is good work. Back in the day, do you know what I did?"

"What did you do?"

"I dug septic systems. I literally dug out people's crap and sucked it up into a tanker truck. And that is honorable."

"Sounds fun," I nodded with a smirk on my face.

"It wasn't. There wasn't anything fun about it, I assure you. But the work was honorable. It made me a better person. Nobody should be ashamed of the work they do. They should do it with pride and do it right. This guy I worked for, the septic guy, he prided himself in doing everything right. It was a great lesson for me. Have you seen somebody's lawn after they have had their septic tanks worked on or replaced? It's a mess, man. It is crazy, like somebody got buried back there. Not the guy I worked for. This guy had us scrape the grass off of the lawn, put it in the back of the truck, exactly like it was when it was on the lawn, then we dug out the septic, putting every shovel full of dirt in the truck so we wouldn't spill dirt all over the lawn, then we emptied the tank and ran a pipe down to the tank, so the next time we had to empty it we didn't have to chew up the lawn. Then we put the dirt back, but there is always too much dirt, because of the pipe, so we had to get a tamper out and tamp the dirt down so it would be level. Then we set the grass back on the dirt, exactly as it had been. I am telling you, Don, nobody ever knew we were there. We did it perfectly. We would get calls every day from people wondering when we were going to be out, and we had to explain we had already been there. People on their cordless phones would argue with us, would yell at us to come and get it done, and we would have to prove to them we had been there. They couldn't believe it."

"That's crazy," I said.

"Yeah, but it is honorable. It taught me to take great pride in what I do, to offer people more than what they expect, to do work as unto the Lord. This guy was a Christian, the guy I worked for, and he told us that everything we do is an act of worship to God, even if it is, literally, sucking people's crap out of a tank in the ground. This was worship to him."

"I've never thought of it that way," I said.

"But do you see what I mean, about life being about God? When it is about God, it makes sense, it gives us a reason for doing what it is we do, beyond even feeding our families. It is bigger even than that."

"Work is worship," I repeated under my breath.

"Yeah," John confirmed. "So that means this: When I don't want to get out of bed, to go and shoot this creation God made, that means there is a God-problem in my life. It means I have to figure out what is going on between me and God that I need to deal with. Everything comes back to my relationship with God."

"You don't think of work as punishment at all?" I asked, wondering out loud if he really meant all this.

"Absolutely not," John said. "I mean, you can cheat or you can build something that doesn't honor God. That's different. But work, the idea of work, is God's invention, and it is part of our spirituality to do it."

Chapter Thirteen

EDUCATION:
JORDAN AND MINDY'S DOG

I grew up believing I was stupid. Nobody told me, but I knew. I say nobody told me, but my report cards said it, the red ink at the top of every page of homework said it, the frustration on my teachers' faces, all of this. Mom worked days and evenings when I was very young, so my sister and I came home from school to an empty house. We fed ourselves, and I walked the land on which we and several other families rented homes. There was a back pasture with a barn but no horses. There were barbed wire fences, and across the north fence was a field, and across the field was a gas station with a store. You could get gum for a nickel. I never did any homework in the evening, and when my mother came home, tired and wanting to watch television, I would lie and tell her I had studied.

I had a terrible case of attention deficit disorder that made it hard to concentrate on anything for more than a few seconds. When listening to a teacher give a talk, I felt I was on a merry-go-round, hearing every fifth sentence. The rest of the time I wondered how dolphins talked under water, or what a civilization of puppets would use as currency.

A person who believes he is stupid is worse than a person who is stupid. My friends Mindy and Jordan have a large dog who submits to a skinny cat. The dog is a pit bull, higher than my knee, muscle all down its hind, hard to the touch on its breastplate. The cat shows bones and whines like a hobo. But the dog does as the cat suggests, because it does not know it is a dog, it does not believe it has any muscle.

All of this is about belief, I suppose. Like I was saying, when you think you're stupid, you act stupid. My school-work consisted of getting by. Each year was about survival. I survived the day, the bully students, the teacher, my mother's inquiries. The idea there was something more than survival never occurred to me. I did not know I could make good grades, or there was a world to learn about, or such a joy as learning. Everybody was frustrated with me, and I felt the Ds and Fs were the bottom of boots kicking me into a hole, and I never thought I could come out, never thought I had the mind to claw and scrape. And so I rolled left when the boot came down, and rolled right when it came down again.

More than 70 percent of students who drop out of school come from fatherless homes. Reading this statistic from the National Principals Report a few weeks ago came as no surprise. With no father to ground the home, the mother works and is exhausted, and is in no way free to nurture and support. I don't believe the sinful nature can be summed up easily, but I know part of it means a person left alone doesn't grow or get strong, not emotionally anyway, and certainly not academically. We all need to be pushed. I didn't get pushed a whole lot, not with the four hands of parents, anyway. God knows a teacher has her mind distracted, kids loud with profanity, and she doesn't feel affirmed by the student who just can't comprehend. And I don't mean to blame everybody else, because I was the one who didn't study, and I was the one who didn't learn. But social conditions matter, otherwise fathers and teachers and mothers are of no consequence.

All that to say the conditions were ripe to teach me I was stupid. And that was one of the few lessons I learned well. Grades, then, became labels. They could almost be considered price tags for my worth.

I never made anything above a C until my senior year in high school. Coming into my senior year, I didn't know if I was going to graduate. My Spanish teacher allowed me into the twelfth grade on the condition I would never take another Spanish class again, for the rest of my life. It is a promise I have kept, but at the time the condition offered no confidence I could lean out across the finish line in subjects involving teachers less gracious.

I recall an evening when I was in high school, having failed another test, lying on my pillow watching the blades of my ceiling fan twirl and wondering whether or not I was mildly retarded. I know it almost sounds humorous, but it's true. That actually happened to me.

But all of this changed the second semester of my senior year. A girl I liked enrolled in a class called Honors Psychology. I went to the school guidance counselor to have my schedule changed.

"This class is only for students in the top 10 percent," she said to me, lipstick on her teeth.

"I didn't know that," I told her. "And where am I?" I asked, glancing at the file on her desk.

"Well," she said, opening the file and pulling out my transcript, "you are not in the top 10 percent. You are definitely in a percentage, but it isn't the top 10 percent."

"What do I need to get into the top 10 percent so I can take that class?" I asked.

"A time machine," she said, being completely serious.

"A time machine?" I asked.

"Right. You could use it to go back in time so you could start over and take school seriously." As she said this, she closed my folder and set it on her desk.

"You don't want to let me into that class, do you?" I asked.

"I can't. The class is for students in the top 10 percent. I'm sorry about this."

"There is nothing you can do?" I asked again.

"Work on your grades, Don. There is no reason your senior year can't be great. Then you can make up for some of this in college."

"Right," I said, standing up and putting on my jacket. I stood in her doorway and wondered about something she had said. I rattled some loose change in my pocket.

"Can I help you with anything else?" she asked. I stood there for a few more seconds, not really talking.

"What is it, Don?" she asked, picking up my file and sliding it into the file cabinet.

"There's no such thing as a time machine, is there? You were kidding, right?" I asked, sort of looking at the ground. She paused, looking at me in shock.

"I was kidding, Don. Yes," she said, shaking her head in amazement.

"Right, then," I told her. "I knew you were kidding. So was I. Okay, nice talking to you. Have a nice day." And with that I walked out as quickly as possible. I walked across the hall, though, and made an appointment with the principal. He happened to be available right away and ushered me into his office.

"What can I help you with, Don?" he asked, a very big and friendly man with a model sailboat on his desk.

"I want to take Honors Psychology," I told him.

"But that class is for students in the top 10 percent. You aren't there, are you?" He asked, wondering if he had my reputation mixed up with somebody else's.

"No, I'm not. It's just that it's been hard, you know, to study and all. I know I haven't done well. But for whatever reason, I want to take this class. Can you get me in?"

"Well, son, I like your ambition. I really do. But I don't think I can do that. It's a special class for special people, and it's not that you're not special, you are. You are very special—"

"Look, Mr. Martindale," I interrupted. "I would like nothing more than to have a time machine and go back in time to take school seriously. Because school is serious. Both you and I know that. But something you and I both also know is there is no such thing as a time machine. I'm smart enough to know that. And so are you. But I feel it, Mr. Martindale." I put my hand to my heart as I said this. "I feel it very deep. I love Honors Psychology. I ache for it. And if you could get me into that class, and perhaps get me a seat next to Nicole Locker, then you would be saying to the whole world there is always a second chance."

"I don't think the world is that interested, Mr. Miller," Mr. Martindale said. And then he did something that surprised me, to this day. He asked his secretary to bring him the student list for the class, and after inspecting it to find only ten students had signed up, he wrote my name on the list. To this day, I don't know why he did it. But I had never been so excited in my life. I was going to learn every-thing there was to know about Nicole Locker, and Honors Psychology too.

Mr. Higbee was the teacher. A former Methodist minis-ter turned agnostic philosopher, he taught the class unlike any other class at the school. He taught it like a college class. We were asked to listen to lectures, weeks and weeks of lectures, and then we were tested. But we were not asked to regurgitate answers we had memorized, we were asked to think. We were asked to recall what we had learned, and to expand, to write how we felt about it, what we agreed with and disagreed with. And to my surprise, after two weeks I had lost interest in the girl, but gained an odd affection for dead personality theorists. Every two months when we were tested I would write and write and write until Mr. Higbee would have to take the pen out of my hand and scoop up the pages from my desk. I was always the last student to leave. I loved the class. And to my amazement, indeed to the amazement of Mr. Higbee and Mr. Martindale, I finished with a 99 percent. Only the valedictorian beat my score.

It was this class that planted the seed of doubt, that maybe I was not mildly retarded, but perhaps one of those special kids who can't speak very well but can play Mozart on the piano. Only I *could* talk, and my Mozart was stuff from a psychology textbook, only I didn't know it super well, just kind of well.

And although I realized later that year I was not

autistic and had no hidden talents of any kind, I also realized, perhaps I was not stupid. And the seed of doubt about my assumed stupidity that started in Mr. Higbee's class gave way to another important realization. Back then, to wind down at night, I was in the habit of going on long walks around the neighborhood. And on a particular night it hit me, and it hit me like a meteor that had fallen from the sky: *I could be anything I wanted.* More specifically it occurred to me that I could be a lawyer, which is ridiculous because I could never be a lawyer. But the deeper truth persisted, and still does today, that there wasn't a glass ceiling above my head, that if I wanted to go out and make something of myself, I could. I know this all sounds silly, and that most people realize this when they are children, but when you grow up hard, there is a part of you that believes life, college, a good job, money, all of this, is for somebody else, and you are not invited to that party.

I would love to say the struggle ended that night, but it didn't. It was a great night, but the going was still rough. Most of my friends went off to college, and because we didn't have any money, and because I hadn't applied myself in school, college didn't feel like an option. I know now that it was. I might have taken a few more years to graduate, but in the long run, this would hardly have set me back. At the time, it was difficult not to compare my life with the life of my friends, almost all of whom went off to school, lived in dorms, went to their college football games, and stayed up all night getting drunk at parties. But I lived at home, delivering Chinese food at night and taking classes in the morning, and I couldn't help feeling like a loser.

But that's when I learned about reading. I'm not proud of this, but it wasn't until I was twenty years old that I read my first book. I'm not kidding. I made it all the way through high school without reading much of anything, and certainly without reading anything cover to cover. But I had this friend, this pen pal who loved poetry, and for her birthday I went into a bookstore and got her a book of poems. The book was *Selected Poems & Letters of Emily Dickinson.* I'd never heard of the author before, but I thumbed through the poetry section at Barnes & Noble until I came across a female name. I flipped open the book and read a few lines, a letter the poet had written to her brother when she was only thirteen. And I was struck. I was struck at the beauty and muscle the young writer employed. She could pack more into a sentence than I could fit into a lifetime of rambling. I sat down in a chair and read half the book before finally getting up and paying for it. I wrote an inscription to my pen pal, wishing her a happy birthday, but I never sent her the book. Each day I would go to put it in an envelope but would read a few pages, then sit down to read the entire book again. I must have read the book fifty times. That pen pal and I became good friends, and after moving to the Pacific Northwest where she lived, she took "her" book off my shelf, claiming that though it was weathered and torn, it belonged to her, proving it by reading aloud the inscription I had written so many years before. I conceded and let her have the book, but got to missing it so much I broke into her house and stole it only a month later, and still have it on my shelf today.

I say this because something important happened to me when I read Emily Dickinson. I fell in love with books. Some people find beauty in music, some in painting, and some in landscape, but I find it in words. By beauty, I mean the feeling you have suddenly glimpsed another world, or looked into a portal that reveals a kind of magic or romance out of which the world has been constructed, a feeling there is something more than the mundane, and a reason for our plodding. The portal is different for everyone. Many of my friends find it by studying physics or math, some from biology or music, but for me it has become literature.

As a by-product of reading, my vocabulary began to improve, and I was able to engage in conversations with friends who had attended school. I don't think there is any substitute for a college education, and I regret not attending myself, but a diligent commitment to reading will get you far. All leaders read, and there are almost no exceptions.

I moved to Oregon in my early twenties where a friend's father offered me a job in his publishing company. I intended to finish college in Oregon, but after securing the job in publishing, I realized I loved the work and was gaining more experience toward a career in books than I would at a university, so I put off school. One year gave to another, and before long I was running the company, and school seemed an afterthought. I am grateful for my friend's father, because he trained me in a profession I love and am grateful to work within every day. But I also knew I had missed out on a liberal education.

That's when I discovered a person could audit classes at nearly any school in the country for a fraction of the cost of enrolling. I'm not recommending this as a substitute for gaining a degree, but if you want to keep learning, it's an option. I've taken classes on the humanities, on literature, on writing, and in theology. I think it's a good idea to take a class every year. Even though John MacMurray teaches at a local Bible college, for instance, he still audits theology classes, just to stay sharp. And I have another friend who created a "Doctorate of Jesus" degree in which he audited dozens of classes from several different universities in the Portland area. When he completes his self-created degree, he won't be able to get a job anywhere, but he will definitely know a lot about Jesus.

I don't think I am stupid anymore. These days, I just think of the mind as a muscle, and by working it, we get more enjoyment out of life. I had a teacher in high school named Mr. Sleepak. He was our music instructor, and he used to tell us if we were coasting, we were moving downhill. He said this to get us to practice our instruments, but I think it's true in all of life. What I mean is, if we aren't learning, we are forgetting, if we aren't getting smart, we are becoming dull.

The latest statistic is that the average American watches 1,456 hours of television a year but only reads three books. So if it's true that readers are leaders, and the more you read the further you advance, then there isn't a lot of competition.

———

BUT IN THE end, I have to tell you the truth. I don't think reading to get ahead is that great of an idea. It's okay, but it's not great. I didn't know *why* a person should read and commit to learning for a long time. It wasn't until I turned thirty that I understood, not till after I had some success, had achieved some goals and realized they didn't mean much. It was then I understood *why* we should learn. I used to believe a person should read books so that when he or she runs for president, he or she would not sound like an idiot before the American people. But this isn't the reason we should educate ourselves, it turns out. I learned why we should learn from Annie Dillard's *Pilgrim at Tinker Creek*. My friend Posie told me about the book, and said she had to read it slowly, that she kept it in the top drawer of a desk and pulled it out like secret chocolate, reading a paragraph at a time, then slipping the book back into the desk to meditate. She spoke about the book as though it were an old lover. I told her I would buy a copy of my own, and she looked at me as though I were about to find faith. The book was indeed rich, and I suspect Posie read a mouthful at a time because the mind was not meant to digest so much so fast. Dillard wrote the book in her twenties, and won the Pulitzer Prize for the effort. It's not a story, but reflections on the heavy surface of the earth: the life in a stream, arteries on a leaf, the wet shine of a turtle's shell coming out of blue-green water. The world falls away as the words combine, and the reader gains the peaceful frenzy of worship. Dillard loves life, and wants to know everything. She learned the names of the flowers and the grasses, not because she wanted to run for president, but because the earth had reached up and grabbed her hand, pulling her low to press her palm against the breathing soil. I felt in reading her we do not read books to learn, we do not learn to succeed, we learn because in doing so we experience something like the pleasure God felt in the act of creation. We discover His handiworks *with* Him.

———

MY FRIEND GREGG used to teach teachers, and he states emphatically that students who are driven by delight will learn more than those driven by discipline. I take this to mean we should move to other subjects if we don't find ourselves enamored. Literature, theology, and psychology fascinate me, and so I consider the subjects a calling. This is my Tinker Creek. While I find a salamander boring, syntax stops my heart. And I wonder how many people think they are dumb when they are not, think academia is for others when it is for everyone. I wonder, when I meet a person who spends their life in front of a television, about the Tinker Creek they never discovered, and where the creek might have taken them, to what heights, to what worship.

Chapter Fourteen

SPIRITUALITY:
AN EDUCATION TOWARD EMPATHY

I don't think the reason I am a spiritual person is because I want to be fathered. This isn't what led me to spirituality, to believing in the Bible. I like the fact I am fathered by God, but what led me to spirituality was a desire to believe I was human, and that being human mattered.

It's a thing with people in general, not to believe they are human. It's a universal struggle, I think. In a way, John and I have done a disservice in this book. Because we've highlighted the fights of the fatherless person, we've led the reader to believe he is alone in a world of well-adjusted people, but nothing like this is true. If you sit down with your friends to scratch the skin, you'll find the same blood as yours, the same decaying bone, the same issues: the girl issues, the athlete issues, the spoiled brat issues. There's a whole catalog an infant can choose from in the womb.

Sometimes a human life can seem no more meaningful than a fish flopping on a shore. Writhing. Out of its element. And I would love to tell you my spirituality battles this perspective, that the real problem in life is we *believe* we are writhing when we aren't, but it isn't true. My spirituality, that is Christian spirituality, does not tell me to close my eyes and pretend life is beautiful and there are no problems to confront. I am told, instead, I am out of water, and finding water again will require a different kind of water. I am told something happened a long time ago and you and I and John and everybody else were washed up on the shore. We will have issues, we will have brokenness.

John would explain the brokenness we experience, the brokenness that mingles in our DNA, is a kind of fallout from the fall of man, that man was made to be in relationship with God but chose his own way, and God let him go, because at some point this is what love has to do. It's fitting then that you and I understand the Fall in a metaphorical way. Because we were separated from our earthly fathers, we know it affects who we have become.

The Scripture that states, *if an earthly father knows how to provide for his children, how much more God knows how to provide for His,* speaks volumes in antithesis too: *If an earthly father abandons his children and wrecks their lives, how much more would an abandonment from God destroy a human being?* As I look at humanity, I can only describe the human personality as one designed for relationship with something from which it has been separated. I hear this rift in conversations, read it in books, listen to it in music, interpret it through psychology, and so on and so on. The idea of this separation has come to feel obvious to me. And perhaps I mean that as a confession, a kind of lens I see the world through that robs me of objectivity. Kindly forgive. I needed the reality when the fantasy stopped working.

But this leaves us in a quandary, doesn't it? A problem for you and me is that our fathers abandoned us. And to come to you and say it wasn't only your father who left, but God too, would be unkind. But that's how it feels. The only bright side, if it could be considered bright, is that we are not alone. A million fish flop alongside us.

This is where John would want to explain why life feels as it does, and ask us to believe we have not been abandoned by God. God is not like our fathers, apparently; He did not leave because He was fed up with us. Nor did He slowly fade from our lives because He found something better to occupy His interest. It is the human race He cares about, every one of us who walked away from our Maker. In Jesus' words, He is like the anxious Father of the prodigal son, longing for us to return. Not because He is some emotionally weak God who needs affirmation from His creation, but because He so thoroughly loves us. And when we don't return, He is like the Great Shepherd of our souls who goes out seeking us, even the one lost sheep.

——

SINCE I LEFT John and Terri's house and moved downtown, John and I would hang out only a couple times a year. We no longer went to the same church, and so I would see him only when we decided to have lunch, or I showed up at one of his seminary classes. Writing this book has been a great blessing because I've seen him nearly every month. We spend the first half hour catching up, John always talking about the kids, about how fast Chris can run and how beautiful the girls are becoming. He tells me Terri is doing well and his dad has moved into the house and they have a new dog. Then we talk about how my writing is coming, not only on this book but in general. We talk about the church I attend, the girl I am dating, the books I am reading. We are slow to get to work, but eventually we get to some bit of theology we need to hash out.

Our last meeting was two weeks ago. I went out to his place and had breakfast. Terri makes a famous Saturday morning breakfast, and it all reminded me of the first weekend I stayed in their house. We ate and I caught up with the kids, and then John said we should meet up in the apartment. Since I left, the space had been set up for Terri's parents, who visit often enough to merit a room.

"It's a lot cleaner now than when you lived here, Don," John said as we rounded the top step. He was right. Terri's mother's furniture was an improvement from my ratty couch and old chair. As I walked around I remembered the piles of clothes and recalled the days when Chris tromped up the stairs to wake me in the morning. I went into the kitchen and could see in my mind the stacks of dishes in the sink, the boxes that I stacked in the hallway, too lazy to walk them down to the garage for storage.

"It even smells nice," I said.

"We had to hire a crew after you moved out. It took a few months of work, but we finally fumigated and got the smell out," John said with a smile.

"Hey, I've changed," I defended.

"I know you have. I know you have," John said.

"You know, John, I remember you coming up one day and saying I would change. You looked around at the piles of clothes and said there would come a day when I couldn't live like that anymore. You were right."

"I thought you'd grow up, Don. Not everyone does."

John and I finally sat down and started talking about this last chapter. We both knew the subject would be spirituality, and wondered where we would go, what we would talk about. You should know John grew up with a father who didn't leave his family. We all call him Papa Mac and he has been living in the house since Hurricane Katrina blew through Louisiana and Mississippi. John flew to Mississippi, where Papa Mac lived, and explained he had to pack whatever he could in the rental car because he couldn't stay through the storm. Papa Mac loaded a few items, an old coin collection, some clothes, and the two of them escaped only hours before the hurricane came ashore. In the end, Papa Mac's house was spared, but he did not go back home. His hearing is nearly gone, and John didn't want him to live alone, so they converted the kids' playroom into a bedroom, and he lives in the house with the MacMurrays now.

I say all this because I knew John wouldn't understand, experientially, what I wanted to write about in regard to God. The feeling a person who grows up without a father has is that God is disinterested. It's a difficult feeling to explain, because I also believe God is loving and good and involved. But there is a doubt, you know, a feeling He is somehow removed. It was the one last issue I wanted to discuss.

"I think the occasional doubt is that God is more interested in other things, other people, perhaps," I stated.

"Is that how you feel about God?" John asked.

"A little. Sometimes."

"And you connect that doubt with the fact you grew up without a dad."

"Yeah. It's nothing I would have recognized before, but it's true. There are times when I don't see God as much different from my friends' fathers when I was a kid. In the end, He has a family of His own to deal with. He's like a good mentor, and I see Him at church."

"Well," John said, "that's interesting, and it is certainly understandable."

"It's not a faith crisis," I clarified. "It's a feeling I get sometimes."

"Yeah, because I know you really believe God is fathering you."

"It's a contradiction, I know. I also know that to the degree I've stuck with Him, sort of given Him the benefit of the doubt, He's blessed my life. He's taken care of me."

"I think that's awesome, Don. Do you know the reason God is fathering you? The reason He does what He does? It's because He is *not* disinterested. The Scriptures use the word *hesed*, which is a Hebrew word we usually translate 'faithfulness.' Essentially, it means *loyal love*."

"Loyal love," I repeated. "And I believe that, you know. I do. I believe God's character is good. It's just . . ."

"It's just you feel like you are a burden on Him," John said. I nodded my head to say yes.

"That's understandable. That's the message you got from your father. But you have to know, Don, He isn't burdened. He delights in us. He champions the cause of the fatherless and the widows."

"Yes, and I know that intellectually, and even somehow believe it. But there are times when it feels like He has withdrawn."

"You know, Don, I think it would be tough for you to

not struggle with that feeling. And the fact you can't see God and talk with Him, like you and I are talking, probably makes it tougher still. But God loves listening to our prayers," John stated. "He loves listening to us talk more than we love talking to Him. Scripture says God delights in the prayers of His children. And the thing about you and me is we can believe things that aren't true. I mean, we can believe them deep in our bones. So, I think the first thing any of us needs to do is to learn to trust that when God says He loves to hear us talk to Him, we believe what He says and we act out of that belief."

"So you just tell yourself to believe?" I questioned.

"Yes and no. I mean, it's more than that. It's not just self-talk. I see Him in creation, my family, my brothers and sisters in my spiritual family, all that. But we also, in a way, build faith intentionally. Think about the psalms of David. David wonders out loud where God is, often accusing Him of abandoning him, and when he meditates and rehearses the truth, he knows in his soul it *is* the truth, and he returns to faith. But, you know, Don, if it stays in your head it will never work. We have to live it out. And that, in turn, increases our faith. It's like any relationship, you have to dive in, you have to let the relationship change you. We do that by obeying God. We submit to Him like a kid does with a father. Scripture says if we love God we will obey God. Our occasional failures or our repeated messes don't negate the truth of that. It's cause and effect. Many people turn it around and it becomes like a dysfunctional father-and-son relationship. We obey because we don't want to get in trouble. We obey because we want Dad's approval. We try to make obedience the cause and love the effect, but it doesn't work. We will eventually bag the whole thing. Love comes first."

"Do you think those feelings will linger — the feelings of doubt?" I asked.

"No, Don, I don't. I mean, you may have them occasionally, but you know, it's like with my kids. They learn to trust me. I tell them I am going to do something, then I follow through, and their trust grows. It's like that with God. You trust Him more now than you used to, don't you?"

"Yeah."

"And that will grow. You're young, with a lot of life ahead. I think the important thing to remember is what you already know, and that is to trust Him, to believe Him, to give Him, as you said, the benefit of the doubt, or as I would say, to have faith. The doubt will decrease."

"That would be good. I think that would be freeing," I said.

"Yeah, no kidding. But you know, Don, I think we are all looking for this quick fix, but relationships don't work that way. We step into them in faith, and they grow stronger, and they change us."

I pondered what John said for a minute. Then I clarified, as if to ask for affirmation one last time: "So, God isn't disinterested? He isn't busy with other things?"

"Not at all. Not the God of Scripture, Don." John said this with a knowing smile.

"Not even sometimes?" I smiled back.

"Not since you learned to clean your room," John stated, straight-faced for a second, then cracking a smile. "Don't put that in the book," he warned.

———

JOHN AND I wrapped up our conversation that evening, and in so doing had our last meeting regarding the book. As we went back into the main house, John told me he wanted to get together every month or so to keep talking. I told him it wasn't necessary, that I had everything I needed to complete the book. I confess I was delighted to hear him laugh and say it had nothing to do with the book—he only wanted to know how I was doing, to keep the friendship going. It meant the world to me. I said good-bye to Terri and the kids and Papa Mac, and I told John I would give him a call. As I walked to the car I looked around the place, out at Mount Hood, up at my old bedroom window. It's true I didn't feel like the same person I was when I lived there. Everything John had said God would do, He did. He was bringing me into maturity. And on the long drive home I kept thinking about the fact God had never abandoned me, and I took comfort in the facts of Scripture. I am not saying

I don't still struggle with these things, because I do. I guess I just struggle less.

———

BUT I KEPT wondering about that initial question: How could God allow such difficult things to happen? You and I know the wound of growing up without a father, but I am talking about all the other wounds, all the other hardships human beings face, many of them so much more painful than ours.

A balm on the wound of that question came through a book I had been reading called *Country of My Skull* by Antjie Krog. The book is about the Truth and Reconciliation Commission in South Africa. The TRC was a commission established by Nelson Mandela to listen to and attempt to reconcile the country after the atrocities of apartheid. It was a sobering account, a group of men and women listening to their countrymen, endless hours of testimony so gripping and gruesome as to beget feelings of hopelessness.

Even as I read, though, I knew God was speaking to me through the pages. Before the commission was established, government officials asked Bishop Desmond Tutu what sort of person should be considered for a position on the commission, and Tutu responded, essentially, that the commission should be comprised of victims, of people whose lives had been ripped open by the horrors of oppression. But not arrogant victims, he stated, not people looking for vengeance. Instead, Tutu said softly, these should be people who have the authority of awful experiences, experiences that educate them toward empathy, and yet still have within themselves hearts willing to forgive. This, he went on to clarify, could be accomplished only through a deeply buttressed spiritual life. These people will be wounded healers.

And I had heard the term before: Wounded Healer. Yet I had never applied the term to my life. It makes you wonder, doesn't it, whether or not God calls specific people who have specific pain into the authority of empathy? Experience is, after all, the best education. We are the ones who will wrestle with security, who will overcome our fear of intimacy, who will learn the hard task of staying with a woman and our children, who will mentor others through the difficult journey of life, perhaps rescuing them from what we have been rescued.

I knew, even as I read Antjie Krog's book, that if these people in South Africa who had suffered unconscionable wrongs could rise in dignity, God would expect nothing less from you and me, having encountered lesser pain. And I think Bishop Tutu's insight is a fitting thought with which to close this book. If John and I have a prayer for you and for the millions who have been abandoned by fathers, it is that we would not be arrogant victims, but wounded healers.

I can only perceive this as a dignified calling.

ACKNOWLEDGMENTS

John and I wish to thank the people at NavPress who were remarkable in their patience and assistance in getting this book together; thanks to Nicci Hubert, Steve Parolini, Don Simpson, Dan Rich, Terry Behimer, Darla Hightower, Arvid Wallen, and Pat Reinheimer.

John, thank you for the great pleasure. Sitting and talking with you, knowing you had better things to do with your time, I can only accept as a gift of grace. I can't repay you, but I will pass the kindness on to somebody else, which I suspect is all you want. Also special thanks to Terri, Chris, Elle, and Cassy MacMurray, who let me live in their home, and who accepted me as a member of their family. God is good, and you are all the evidence we need.

It is hard to imagine a person doing a better job of expressing love in the face of difficulty more than my mother. I didn't write much about Mom in this book, because she is a book of her own. After my sister and I left home, my mother, in her fifties, enrolled in night school and earned both her bachelor's and master's degrees. Mom, you are the greatest role model a person could have, and I am deeply grateful.

Special thanks to David Gentiles, Tara Brown, Jordan Green, David Allen, Jim Chaffee, Kathy Helmers, Rick McKinley, Tony Kriz, Kurt and Donna Nelson, Kaitie Nelson, Randy Alcorn, Jeff Foxworthy, Ernie Johnson, Tim Cash, Leonard and Elizabeth Sweet, Blake Gaskill, Grant Gaskill, Greg Spencer, and Gregg Harris for your help and encouragement. And to Dan, Matt, Charlie, and Stephen for letting me come on the road and read portions of the book to your great audiences. Nobody should receive that kind of honor. And thanks to John Eldredge, whose Wild at Heart Boot Camp provided a healing experience necessary to dive further into these issues.

As I wrote, I listened to Derek Webb's new record *Mockingbird*, Sara Groves, Jars of Clay, U2, Johnny Cash, Lyle Lovett, Gary Jules, Ray Charles, Bob Schneider, Ryan Adams, Dan Bern, Willie Nelson, Jeff Buckley, Ben Harper, The Waterboys, Mark Knopfler, Mogwai, Kanye West, The Alarm, Big Head Todd, Audioslave, The Blind Boys of Alabama, Beck, and Bruce Springsteen.

BOCA

TICKETING TECHNOLOGY BY

SHUBERT TICKETING SERVICES

A DIVISION OF THE
SHUBERT ORGANIZATION, INC

N- 3927975

Your direct connection to the box office

Telecharge.com

Telecharge.com
Group Sales
212-239-6262 / 800-432-7780

or tickets and information, visit us online or call 212-239-6200

N- 3927975

212-239-6262 / 800-432-7780

AMAJPH
032906D

$90.00

TV
031406
ORCHO

0   5

MAJESTIC THEATRE
245 W. 44TH ST. N.Y.C.

THE PHANTOM
OF THE OPERA

2:00 PM WED
MAR 29, 2006

XAWEB1374-0314-Y108S

THIS TICKET IS NONREFUNDABLE

BIELENBERG, DANIEL R

AMAJPHO32906D
961393595130

$90.00

TAVISA TV

ORCHO

0   5

Thanks to you for reading this book. It means the world, and we are grateful. John and I have similar jobs in that we try to capture what God does, getting it down on paper, and without you we'd have to get real jobs, driving buses or ferry boats, and that would put people in danger.

John and I have dedicated this book to men who mentor younger men. Thank you for the time you put in, your concern, your patience and prayers. The impact you make brings healing in ways you may never understand. Much appreciation to you, and all God's blessing.

ABOUT
THE AUTHORS

DONALD MILLER is the founder of The Belmont Foundation, a foundation committed to aiding single mothers and providing mentors for fatherless kids, and is the director of *The Burnside Writers Collective*, an online magazine that occasionally changes and aims to provide reading material for people who are supposed to be working. He is the author of *Blue Like Jazz, Searching for God Knows What*, and *Through Painted Deserts*. He lives and works in Portland, Oregon.

JOHN MACMURRAY has a master's degree from Western Seminary and has taught the Bible for over twenty-five years.

For nearly two decades, he has made his living as a landscape nature photographer. His images have appeared in *National Geographic, Sierra Club, Audubon,* and several other publications. John lives in the Pacific Northwest with his wife, Terri, and their three children, Chris, Elle, and Cassy. John's photography can be found in his two books: *By Chance? Landscapes from the Canvas of the Creator* and *The Call of Creation: Nature's Invitation to Worship.*

For more information about the authors, please visit:
   Donald Miller: www.donaldmillerwords.com
   John MacMurray: www.creationcalendars.com

Another site of interest:
   www.burnsidewriterscollective.com

Check out the I-Mix on I-Tunes called "To Own a Dragon" for a playlist Don chose while wrapping up the book.

THE BELMONT FOUNDATION
www.belmontfoundation.org

63% of youth suicides are from fatherless homes –
5 times the average. (U.S. Dept. of Health/Census).

85% of all children who show behavior disorders come from
fatherless homes – 20 times the average. (Center for Disease Control)

80% of rapists with anger problems come from fatherless homes –
14 times the average. (Justice & Behavior, Vol. 14, p. 403-26)

71% of all high school dropouts come from fatherless homes –
9 times the average. (National Principals Association Report)

75% of all adolescent patients in chemical abuse centers come from
fatherless homes – 10 times the average. (Rainbows for All God's Children)

70% of youths in state-operated institutions come from fatherless
homes – 9 times the average. (U.S. Dept. of Justice, Sept. 1988)

85% of all youths in prison come from fatherless homes –
20 times the average. (Fulton Co. Georgia, Texas Dept. of Correction)

The Belmont Foundation is Donald Miller's not-for-profit organization that exists
to provide role models for children growing up without fathers. To learn more
about what you can do to help, please visit www.belmontfoundation.org.